WEALTH

DAVID OSBORN AND PAUL MORRIS

CAN'T

BEGIN YOUR FUTURE TODAY!

WAIT

GREENLEAF
BOOK GROUP PRESS

This publication is designed to provide accurate and authoritative information in regard to the subject matter covered. It is sold with the understanding that the publisher and author are not engaged in rendering legal, accounting, or other professional services. If legal advice or other expert assistance is required, the services of a competent professional should be sought.

Published by Greenleaf Book Group Press
Austin, Texas
www.gbgpress.com

Distributed by Greenleaf Book Group

For ordering information or special discounts for bulk purchases, please contact Greenleaf Book Group at PO Box 91869, Austin, TX 78709, 512.891.6100.

Design and composition by Greenleaf Book Group
Cover design by Greenleaf Book Group

Cataloging-in-Publication data is available.

Print ISBN: 978-1-62634-419-8
eBook ISBN: 978-1-62634-421-1
Audiobook ISBN: 978-1-62634-420-4

Part of the Tree Neutral® program, which offsets the number of trees consumed in the production and printing of this book by taking proactive steps, such as planting trees in direct proportion to the number of trees used: www.treeneutral.com

Printed in the United States of America on acid-free paper

17 18 19 20 21 22   10 9 8 7 6 5 4 3 2 1

First Edition

THIS BOOK IS FOR our beloved families, friends, and heroes—our great mentors, teachers, and business partners who cared enough to help us on our journey. This book is for all those who have taught us how to be better people and for those we've had the pleasure of helping. This book is a reflection of all of you. May our collective wisdom change lives for the better.

CONTENTS

PART THREE
CREATE THE HABITS THAT BUILD WEALTH   123

PART FOUR
DEVELOP A BUSINESS THAT BUILDS WEALTH   157

PART FIVE
GENERATE THE MOMENTUM THAT BUILDS WEALTH   205

BUILDING WEALTH

The wealthy do not focus on day-to-day short-term survival.
Successful people focus on wealth building assets.
—Stephen Richards

Some people are born on third base—they inherit money, marry into wealth, or win the lottery. The rest of us must hit base hits (and sometimes strike out) in our journey to build our own wealth. This book is for anyone who wants to put the odds in their favor. In the pages that follow, we'll show you how to adopt the mindset and develop the skills you will need to empower your freedom, create your future, and build a life worth living today.

We're privileged to be a part of an extraordinary company, Keller Williams Realty International, which is the largest real estate company in the world, with 150,000 agents as of this printing. We are Keller Williams's top-selling broker-owners, and we joined forces to write this book so we could share how you can build wealth in *all* areas of your life.

We've divided our book into five parts:

1. Making the Choice to Build Wealth
2. Embracing the Mindset That Builds Wealth

3. Creating the Habits That Build Wealth

4. Developing a Business That Builds Wealth

5. Generating the Momentum That Builds Wealth

Building wealth—as opposed to just having money go through your hands—requires you to make different choices, think different thoughts, practice different habits, and conduct business in a different way. These principles and practices are the same for everyone who is wealthy. And we're going to show you how you can follow these practices in your life so that you can build wealth, just as we have.

Building wealth. These two words work well together. Your level of income doesn't determine your level of wealth. If you're not building wealth, then you're depleting it. Just as you can build muscle, or strengthen tennis skills, or tend your backyard into a wonderful oasis, the minute you stop doing these things your muscle withers, your tennis skills rust, and your garden overgrows.

Just like with these activities, building wealth is a process that requires repetition and consistency to build "muscle." It's an application of knowledge to life that has a built-in feedback loop. When building wealth, you apply your knowledge through effort or investment. When you do this, you produce results and you either win or lose. Then you apply what you learned and do it all over again. Throughout this book, we share the knowledge and tools that will help you create habits that build wealth.

Having lots of money alone means nothing. Former NBA Star Allen Iverson had lots of money and lost it. Lottery winners have lots of money (and many of them end up losing it)—but they could preserve it and grow it if they practice the wealth-building methods in our book. The real journey to wealth, however, is built upon the knowledge, skills, habits, and relationships that you apply to money.

In the pages that follow, we share our journey and the lessons we have learned. These are lessons that people can use to climb their own mountains. If you are going to cure cancer, launch the next Rolling

Stones, or build a new tech start-up and become a billionaire, please drop this book and get after it. Our techniques are not for you. This book is for anyone who wants to put the odds in their favor and to build long-term, sustainable wealth. It's for the man or woman who says, "I want my life to be awesome, unrecognizable from what it is now in five to ten years." It's not about winning the lottery or becoming an instant billionaire.

This book is about building wealth. It will empower you with a set of skills that will serve you for a lifetime. We can help you create a life that is more joyous, one that will enable you to work with some talented people and do some incredible things. We do not have a get-rich-quick formula for you. Instead, we have a wealth-building formula for you. The journey is yours to take. We can't do the work for you. But here's the good news: It doesn't have to be "hard" work. It's play. By practicing what we offer in this book, you will learn to thrive and create the life you desire.

Over the years we have built a lot of wealth, and we continue to do so. We've had things go our way and go against us. Our approach will work for you. The greatest thing you can do to increase your wealth is to further your knowledge of wealth. The skills we share here are not just important; they are crucial to building wealth. In this book, you will find the keys that unlock wealth-building potential for anyone with the ambition, energy, and desire to do so.

So, what are you waiting for? Let's get started!

PART

**MAKE THE CHOICE
TO BUILD WEALTH**

ONE

A MATTER OF CHOICE

Every decision you make takes you one step closer
to being wealthy . . . or one step further away.
—Shay Olivarria

Building wealth requires making a choice. One day you wake up. And instead of getting back to the rat race, you stop. You look at your life and ask, "What's going on here?"

Maybe it was a life-changing event, be it positive or negative. Maybe you just picked up this book. It doesn't really matter. Regardless of the reason, it's moments like these that create an opportunity. They create a window of clarity to see your life from the outside in. At these moments you can stop and ask yourself, "Is the way I'm choosing to live my life leading me to the future that I really want?"

> " All of us are, to some degree, sleepwalking through our lives."

All of us are, to some degree, sleepwalking through our lives. However, in these reflective moments we have the opportunity to ask ourselves if our lives are truly in line with the lives we would choose if we could have anything we desired.

The Programmed Life

Many of us lead a "programmed life." What we do is determined by our culture, family, values, friends, education, career path, and financial status. For example, Paul's parents thought that education and working as a professional—a lawyer, doctor, or engineer—was the right path for him. Think about it. Maybe your parents were not wealthy, like Paul's, and believed in the value of a good education and a professional career as a doctor or engineer. Twenty years later, you've made your life choices to please your family and follow someone else's notion of what's right for you, but you hate your career. Thinking back on these choices, does it still serve you to live by someone else's rules? Does it even really serve them?

What Really Matters

It is important to know what matters to you in your life. Money doesn't really matter, unless, of course, you don't have any. But when you do have enough money to meet your basic needs, what really matters is what you can do with it. For example, money allows you to give your children the opportunity to get a good education. Money allows you to receive great health care. You can also travel more easily and contribute to great causes when you have money. Sounds like fun, right? And yet money still doesn't matter.

So, what matters then? Everyone's answers will vary, so we encourage you to come to your own conclusions as you ponder this important question. But we're going to give you a hint: It's not money. [[COMP: Insert Figure 1.1]]

Why Wealth Matters

Many people equate wealth to material goods and services, such as cars, houses, and taking lavish vacations. How many times have you heard the phrase, "Money isn't everything"? We agree—somewhat. So, what is wealth then? What value does it have at its core?

When you strip away all your material possessions, any precon-ceived ideas of the "good life," and all your attachments, you're left with three things:

1. Health
2. Family
3. Freedom

Think for a moment: Can money buy you health? Well, it depends who you ask and when you ask them. If you ask former billionaire Steve Jobs, the answer, quite obviously, is "no." He died of pancreatic cancer at the age of 56. No amount of money could have saved his cancer-ridden body. However, if you consider the nearly 800 million people living now who don't have access to clean water or sufficient food, just a little bit of money would "buy" them a lot of health.

Can money buy you time? If you ask a dying man or woman, at most money can buy them only a small amount of time. Money is also not good at buying time that's already lost. But money—if spent well—does buy you future time. For example, Paul's nephew recently rode a bus 26 hours from Chicago to Boston to see his cousin's grad-uation. In this instance, $500 could have bought him a plane ticket home and saved him 20 hours.

Does money buy you family? Again, it depends on whom you ask. If you have a strained relationship with your family, chances are you're going to need to do more than write a check. You'll need to work on rebuilding those important relationships. But if you are an infertile couple looking to adopt a child, money can definitely help you build a family. It's all a matter of perspective. In fact, the more we thought about it, the more we realized that money is synonymous with choice, or, better yet, freedom.

Wealth Brings Freedom

" When you say yes to wealth, you're saying yes to
your potential for freedom."

Freedom is the power to choose and create. When you say yes to wealth, you're saying yes to your potential for freedom. You're acknowledging the power of possibility in your life.

The wealthy are free to express themselves as they truly are—kind and giving or selfish and insufferable. As Will Smith said, "Money and success don't change people; they merely amplify what is already there."

In the absence of wealth, your choices are limited, and we believe this compromises your quality of life, work, and health. Wealth creates freedom, and freedom is the ultimate gift in life.

Building Wealth Is Saying "Yes" to Yourself

The lessons we share with you we learned through personal experience (both wins and losses) and from carefully observing other people and their approaches to building and maintaining not only wealth but also healthy and happy lives.

" Wealth building positively affects your personal
and professional relationships and inspires your
day-to-day outlook."

Wealth building positively affects your personal and professional relationships and inspires your day-to-day outlook. As you choose to embrace wealth and experience greater choice, over time you will feel a sense of heightened calm, satisfaction, and genuine security—and not just of the material variety.

Building wealth is a way of saying "yes!" to yourself and to those things that are important to you. It's a way to align with all that you love and all that inspires you on your journey each day. By adopting a wealthy mindset and practicing the skills we recommend in the chapters ahead, you get to focus on what matters most to you.

WEALTH ACCELERATOR

Wealth is just code for freedom, and freedom is the ultimate gift in life.

Wealth Can't Wait

If anyone suggests that your focus on building wealth is misplaced, just smile, thank them, and wish them luck. You alone are the master of your wealth-building ship. And remember, you can't buy back your time—it's finite. So, make each day count. Commit to wealth and build your bridge to freedom now, because wealth can't wait.

We hope that you'll take the time to contemplate your life as you read this book. And if you don't like what you're doing or how you currently live, know that you can take action now that will produce positive change. We wrote this book to help you create the space and awareness so that you can alter your life in any way you choose.

BONUS CONTENT: JUMPSTART YOUR JOURNEY TO WEALTH

To reward you for taking this wealth-building journey with us, we're giving you some bonus material online. The bonus for this chapter consists of strategic questions to help you get in touch with the life of your dreams. The journey to building wealth begins when you determine what you want and take responsibility for getting there!

By visiting the link below, you will find questions, diag-
nostics, audios, and videos, all designed to jumpstart your
journey to wealth. You can unlock them by going to www.
wealthcantwait.com.

CHAPTER 2

AN ISSUE OF COMMITMENT

The line of progress is never straight.
—Martin Luther King Jr.

Being wealthy, first and foremost, is a state of mind. It requires a commitment to winning the game of wealth. This will require you, at times, to look foolish, feel uncomfortable, be direct, and to purposefully focus your efforts and resources.

So, what does commitment look like?

Commitment is a knowing that permeates your being such that it becomes a part of you. It is a willingness to do whatever it takes. It's a way of weaving that knowing into your fiber so that it goes with you on each step you take every day. If you commit to something 100%, it's virtually certain to happen—unless you change your mind or die. That's how steadfast we can all be in our commitments as we walk around each day. That doesn't mean that we don't take days off, or procrastinate, or have moments of doubt; but our willingness to reignite our long-term vision and our commitment to our journey never wane.

66 Knowledge without action is wasted potential."

To attentively build wealth, make these major commitments:

1. **Save capital to invest.** At almost any income level you can save capital. Ronald Read, a Vermont janitor and gas station attendant proved this well: By spending less than he earned and investing the rest, he ended up saving $8 million over the course of his life!

2. **Make saving a daily habit and revisit your spending and savings goals each month.** By simply mastering the art of saving and investing, you could end up with a fortune the size of Ronald Read's!

3. **Learn about wealth.** You can accomplish this simply by reading or listening to four books a year about investments. Learning consistently leads to greatness over time.

4. **Search for investments in your areas of choice.** It's crucial to hunt down opportunities that produce a solid yield. Hunting is a way of life for an entrepreneur. Keep looking until you find something that helps you win. Hunting will teach you along the way. Once you've found a way to get a good yield and maximize it, find another.

5. **Take action.** Knowledge without action is wasted potential. Follow these steps even when your knowledge is less than complete. The important thing is to stop over-thinking and move!

To maximize your potential, commit to these four activities for the rest of your wealth-building life.

The Only Time You Lose Is when You Quit

What if you fail? Failure doesn't stop you from building wealth. It's actually part of the process. If you don't do something you committed to, then let it go and start over. If you commit to taking action, failing is a certainty. It's part of the journey. So have a short memory and focus on the present and future. Don't let a memory of failure, or success, hold you back.

66 The only time you lose is when you quit."

If you've failed at something—that's OK. It won't matter in the long run. Failure happens all the time, so don't waste time beating yourself up. Get over it, dust yourself off, and get after it again. And remember: The only time you lose is when you quit.

The Upside of Commitment

Commitment has a massive upside. The more you keep your commitments, the better you function in all areas of your life. When you know you keep your commitments with every fiber of your being, it makes it so much easier to accomplish goals that are amazing.

As you develop goal-getting skills and build goal-getting muscle, you get more and more of what you want. And as you get more and more of what you want, guess what happens? Your goals get bigger, your choices get bigger, your vision gets bigger, and your outcomes get bigger. More becomes possible. As shown in the illustration that follows, it's a positive feedback loop of choosing what you want, getting what you want, and deciding to get even more.

WEALTH ACCELERATOR

Develop the skills of goal-setting and commitment to get more of what you want.

Develop the skills of goal-setting and commitment, and you will get more and more of what you want. As you get more of what you want, your passion for life will increase. And as your passion for life increases, you will find that you have the resources and energy to build an even bigger vision. It's a self-reinforcing process.

CHAPTER 3

AVOIDING THE SEVEN WEALTH TRAPS

Be thankful for what you have; you'll end up
having more. If you concentrate on what you
don't have, you will never . . . have enough.
—Oprah Winfrey

To build wealth, you must actively cultivate a can-do, make-it-happen, fully aware state of mind. This will help you avoid the seven wealth traps and make it far easier to reach your goals.

To build awareness and enhance your state of mind, think of someone who is less talented, less hardworking, less smart, and less of whatever it is you are good at, yet has more wealth than you. The odds are that person has escaped the wealth traps. This simple exercise is a great reminder that there's no reason you can't become wealthy, too.

In nearly all things, the biggest obstacle we'll ever face is ourselves. By looking at the seven most common wealth traps, we can learn how to avoid these obstacles and achieve our wealth goals.

Wealth Trap 1: The Stable or Cushy Job

We all know folks like these:

- A ski instructor who loves to ski
- A bartender who enjoys the social part of her job
- A flight attendant who values travel

All of these individuals are getting some subset of their needs met. But is it enough? Are they short-changing themselves? Do they ever think to themselves, "I could be more"? Do they tell themselves they are not living up to their potential? And, do they have to quit their jobs? Not necessarily.

They could still achieve their wealth goals by doing something—even seemingly small—to make a big impact. For example, the skier could look into creating a ski school or becoming a professional coach. The bartender could start saving her tips and explore investing her extra income in rental properties. And the flight attendant could take his savings and open a franchise. All of these scenarios would enable them to embark on the path to wealth and begin to have their money work for them. Along the way, they can use their personal skills to build an incredible network that includes others with similar or complementary interests.

> ❝ Building wealth is a contact sport."

WEALTH ACCELERATOR

You can build a path toward financial freedom outside of work while keeping your job. There are many paths to wealth, but staying comfortable where you are will not get you on them.

Opportunities come every day. It's how we show up and our willingness to see opportunity that determines if our networks will open doors. Building wealth is a contact sport. It requires movement, action, and impact. Be purposeful and build a network that takes you closer to your goals.

Wealth Trap 2: Risk Avoidance

We all fear failure. We want to get it right. That is human nature. Ask yourself, "What is truly at risk?" Will you starve? Will you become homeless? Is your life at risk? Wealth is built alongside some risk. And, the longer you wait, the greater the stakes!

If you take your savings and buy a property—one you can fix up and rent out or sell—what's truly at risk? Do you fear losing those dollars that took you so long to save?

> " The biggest risk in life is not taking one."

Is it ego? Do you think you will get ridiculed for failing? More likely, most people will probably envy you for being bold enough to take such a risk. Compared to other nations, we have fewer people who are starving or are without shelter. Yet most of us sit on the sidelines and overestimate our risk. We're not going to sugarcoat this—building wealth involves taking risks. But it's overinflated compared to the risk of doing nothing. The biggest risk in life is not taking one.

Wealth Trap 3: Viewing Wealth as a Negative

At some level, do you view money as dirty? Do you feel like you have to apologize for wanting to build wealth? Perhaps this perspective would help: Pursuing wealth is pursuing freedom. Think of what you can do with that freedom, the difference you can make when you are financially free. What positive impact could you have on your family, your friends, even on the world at large? Celebrate your pursuit of wealth and look at it as a pathway to freedom. And, steer clear from those who think money is a dirty word.

Wealth Trap 4: Not Staying the Course

The pursuit of wealth, like any path in life, has its ups and downs. You'll win some and lose some. We see people quit way too early. If you take an initial step and then have one bad experience, is it really time to quit? Of course not. Maybe you lose money on an investment or you are held responsible for a loan for a business that failed.

When you face a setback, you have a choice: You can jump ship by focusing on the sting of the loss or stay the course and reap the value of the lesson. Just remember: You had courage before the loss, and now you have the power of more experience and information as you move forward. Wouldn't it be better to profit from that experience and combine it with your action and skills as you stay the course?

WEALTH ACCELERATOR

If you failed, that's okay. Take the lesson and march forward with more experience under your belt.

Wealth Trap 5: The Weak Social Circle

How many people are best friends with their kindergarten buddies? Not many. Yet how many folks have a friend they won't cut loose, even though they are a negative influence?

If we are pursuing our destiny, then friends will come and go. If you are growing and others are not, move on. You can still love them, just see them less. Tell them they are welcome on the journey and move on. Everything has a use-by date and just as old milk will spoil, so too will your social circle.

Wealth Trap 6: The Victim and Negativity Trap

Bad stuff happens every day. Life can be really hard. Unfair things occur. All of this is true. And if you build a house in past misery, move in, and hang pictures on the walls of the sorts of things that happen to you, you could easily get stuck there, maybe even forever!

> " It's hard to move forward with a positive vision when you are locked into an event from the past."

Victimhood leads to blame, apathy, and general malaise. It's hard to move forward with a positive vision when you are locked into an event from the past. Negativity tends to lead to inertia and despondence. Don't let a bad occurrence hold you back.

Wealth Trap 7: The Know-It-All Trap

There is someone who thinks that they know it all in every crowd. As Steven Hawking said, "The greatest enemy of knowledge is not ignorance, it is the illusion of knowledge." On the path to wealth, stay curious. The illusion of knowledge, the expert syndrome, as we refer to it, stops curiosity, hinders teachability, and limits you on your journey.

CHAPTER 4

HAVING COURAGE

Courage is being scared to death,
but saddling up anyway.
—John Wayne

Starting your wealth-building journey is not about what you know. It's about having the courage to dive in and the willingness to learn along the way. Knowledge is one of the most overrated assets in wealth building. Sometimes the more you know, the less likely you are to take the action to build wealth. For example, how many economics professors are wealthy? Yet who knows more about economic forces than an economics expert?

We're not saying don't analyze opportunities. Instead, we're asking you to realize that when you analyze an opportunity, there will almost always be more reasons not to do something than to do it. Our primitive brains are designed to keep us alive by avoiding risk. Unfortunately, this also inhibits action.

It Is Risky, but Start Anyway

When David was building his real estate company, he and his team pitched their concept to many very smart and experienced real estate professionals. The overwhelming majority declined their offer. One guy in particular was an amazing realtor. He worked very hard and produced almost $1 million a year in commission income, netting more than $500,000 a year. He was bright and highly educated in this particular area, and the offices he declined now produce more than $1 million dollars a year in passive income! Today that guy is still at the same grind, working very hard selling real estate. He's still earning about $500,000 a year, but he is older now, and not loving the grind as much as he once did.

Unfortunately, he passed on one of the best opportunities of his lifetime, because it seemed too new and risky. His need for security led him to wait, see how it went, and acquire more information. This play-it-safe approach caused him to miss out on a great opportunity.

At the time we bought our first real estate franchises, we had no idea what we were doing. Though coming from different places, we both took action. What we shared was a willingness, a learning-based mind, and some great mentors. We both took action and planted the seeds for building more wealth with limited information rather than waiting for more sophisticated analysis. It was this willingness to take action and learn from our mistakes and mentors that built most of our wealth.

If You Commit to Building Wealth, It Will Happen

You build wealth by applying yourself to the task of building wealth. If you commit to building wealth, it will happen. It's that simple. The willingness to take action, to fail, to reevaluate, and then keep going is far more important than sitting on a mountaintop contemplating the next big thing. Although, as you will learn later, there is a time to contemplate.

WEALTH ACCELERATOR

Build wealth through the actions you take and the results you get (both positive and negative) rather than the knowledge you start with.

CHAPTER 5

HAVING WEALTH VISION

It takes as much energy to wish as it does to plan.
—Eleanor Roosevelt

Once you decide to be wealthy, the second most important step in building a life of abundance is to create a wealth vision. In other words, now that you've carefully looked at your thoughts, removed the ones that didn't serve you, and seeded the ones that will take you to your goal, your next step is to treat that vision of a beautiful future as if it were present now.

We're created a simple four-part PATH that can take you to your wealth vision:

1. **P**lan for wealth.
2. Take **A**ction steps to move you forward.
3. Work with a **T**eam of talented people and peers.
4. **H**old yourself accountable.

Plan for Wealth

People who build wealth tend to have a plan, a focus, and a vision for the future. Your plan is where you will spend the majority of your thinking time, cultivating a burning desire to achieve it. By choosing this plan, and by committing to it, you will begin to be shaped by the future outcome you have chosen. You become a focused being instead of a wandering generality. Creating your own wealth plan allows you to step into a future that builds wealth. This plan has a clear outcome, method, and model. And it can be modified as circumstances dictate.

Take Action Steps to Move Yourself Forward

Once you have a plan, break it down into action steps that immediately move you toward your chosen outcome. For example—

- If you want to write a novel, thinking about it all day, day after day won't get you there. You must put pen to paper.
- If you want to sell, then you must learn your product and prospect for leads.
- If you want to build a company, then you must learn to lead.

> " Action is the bridge between ideas, potential, and reality."

Action is the bridge between ideas, potential, and reality. A wrong action is better than no action, because then you will then have experience and an opportunity to learn. Life is risky. But it's even riskier if you do nothing. In fact, having the "big idea" is often enough to keep people complacent enough to do nothing. When action is key, an idea can be worthless if it lulls you into inaction.

Work with a Team of Talented People and Peers

People who build wealth quickly and with ease tend to have the ability to surround themselves with amazing, talented folks. We call this leverage, and we cover it in greater detail later in this book. One thing that separates us from the pack is being able to hire the very best people as employees, consultants, coaches, or advisors.

For example, what could you accomplish if you could hire the best of the best to assist you in creating your dreams? Would hiring a world-class assistant accelerate your growth path?

We're amazed when we see people failing to delegate things they don't like doing. If a person is repairing their car, they're trading the hours they could spend building wealth doing work they could easily outsource. The same is true for mowing your yard or cleaning your house. Maybe you feel that you can't afford that right now, or it seems like a luxury. We would say that unless you find it therapeutic to clean your house, you should outsource it and spend that time taking action on your plan.

If you find yourself saying, "But no one does it as well as me," it's time to let that perfectionism go and get out of your own way. The truth is no one will do it *exactly* like you. But think about this: There are also those who could do it even *better*.

So, give outsourcing a try. The more you outsource to others, the more you create an amazing team. And in turn, the more time you will have to take action on, and do, the critical thinking for the business and future you are creating.

> " Delegation and building a phenomenal team is a cornerstone of winning at the highest level."

Delegation and building a phenomenal team is a cornerstone of winning at the highest level. Put your soul into your dream and let others support you on the journey. Great forces come to the aid of those who are willing to get out of their own way and strive for a definite purpose, something that will make a difference and leave a legacy.

We love hiring great people and seeing them win. We've learned that if we can put someone in a position where they thrive and earn more than ever before while enjoying the process, they will be incredibly productive. In turn, our economic world grows with them. What could be a better outcome than that?

> " Planning to build your fortune while planning to build the fortunes of those on your team takes vision, and it is the fastest way to accelerate your own growth."

We view this as a covenant relationship, meaning that if those folks are creating great wealth for us, then we fail if they don't become financially successful as well. Planning to build your fortune while planning to build the fortunes of those on your team takes vision, and it is the fastest way to accelerate your own growth.

Once you change your vision around this, you can immediately look for and attract talent. We're on the constant lookout for talented people we might hire or partner with to create something great. This awareness comes naturally once you have a big vision. For example, take the phenomenal barista you run into: What could you create together? Think about those in your life who have amazing ideas or talents but lack certain skills that you happen to have. Could you partner with these people to build wealth as a team?

There is a flipside to this: Take care to separate yourself from the passive thinkers. You want to be sure you are teaming up with someone who can take action as well as plan. Find someone with an inspirational idea and ask what he or she has created in the past. If it is failure after failure—each of which will no doubt have amazing explanations,

excuses, or blame—then run. Failure without learning—just like success—is contagious.

Hold Yourself Accountable

66 Accountability isn't about blame or finding
wrong. It's about owning your circumstances
and outcomes."

People loathe accountability. It's a dirty word; the very thought of it
causes eye-rolling and trepidation. And yet when we create a different
perspective on accountability, it actually sets us free. There isn't a top
athlete in the world who doesn't either hold themselves accountable,
or have a great coach to hold them accountable for improvement. No
spaceship was ever launched without accountability. No great business
outcomes are achieved without feedback and accountability. Accountability isn't about blame or finding wrong. It's about owning your circumstances and outcomes.

Once you own your circumstances and your outcomes, only then
do you have the possibility of changing them.

Once you adopt this view, this principle of accountability, you'll
find you can use it everywhere. For example, if you want to be a great
skier, hire an Olympic-level coach or one with an exceptional reputation to hold you accountable and teach you. Want to be an awesome
golfer? Hire the best golf coach you can find. Want to learn to prospect
in sales? Hire a sales coach. This can be incredibly fun. A great coach
gets you to do what you don't want to do, so that you can become
what you've always wanted to be. And, a great coach shares new perspective to get you there faster and with more ease. The same is true
of your peers. Choose as friends those who are striving for something
greater. If they are busy living a life that is accountable to their goals,
chances are you will be inspired to do the same.

We have created our own system of accountability by building a tribe of highly successful entrepreneurs to whom we are accountable at our regular mastermind meetings. During these meetings, we serve as a board of directors for one another. Each entrepreneur in our group shares their business plan and gets feedback from other members of the group.

WEALTH ACCELERATOR

Accountability is the breakfast of champions. Use it to push your life to amazing levels of success.

CHAPTER 6

BUILDING GREATER WEALTH NATURALLY

Measurement is the first step that leads to control and
eventually to improvement. If you can't measure something,
you can't understand it. If you can't understand it, you can't
control it. If you can't control it, you can't improve it.
—H. James Harrington

If you think of yourself as a corporation, you will naturally build greater
wealth. For example, Paul's inspiration for creating the corporation ME,
Inc. came from a video that he watched about fifteen years ago that featured coauthor David Osborn. At that time, Paul was in his late thirties
and didn't know David that well. David was talking about how he used
leverage by hiring other people to start Keller Williams offices for him
and to run his business operations. In that video, when David mentioned that he had his own personal chief financial officer, Paul realized
that David ran his entire life like a corporation.

66 If you think of yourself as a corporation, you will
naturally build greater wealth."

David measured everything, including income, expenses, and growth. He set goals like earnings expectations and measured his progress against them. He hired and fired and then hired others who hired and fired. It was something that, though requiring oversight, he could walk away from, and it would still carry on.

By that time, Paul already owned several business entities. After watching David's video, he shifted in mindset and action and formed a corporation called Morris Enterprises, Inc. (ME, Inc.) It was 100% self-owned and did nothing other than serve as a place for all his income and expenses to flow through.

WEALTH ACCELERATOR

At some point in life—when your business grows large enough—the tax and structural benefits outweigh the cost of running a corporation (a minimum of $2,000 a year). That's when you should take this step and form your version of ME, Inc.

You can, however, begin to think of yourself as a corporation immediately. In fact, adopting this mindset will significantly benefit your business. Even if you are an hourly wage earner, your household generates income and incurs expenses. For example, you save, spend, and have the opportunity to invest.

Following are some questions to get you started. This purposeful inquiry will set you on a path to build wealth regardless of your answers. That is because these questions bring awareness, and awareness can incite change. For example, start asking yourself—

- How much does your household earn a year?
- What are the sources of your household income?

- What is your net income after taxes?
- How much do you spend on essentials?
- How much do you spend on leisure or discretionary spending?
- How much could you invest?

Once you've answered these questions, you can take these three basic steps to begin treating yourself like a corporation:

1. Learn how to create a profit-and-loss statement.
2. Track your expenses each month.
3. Create a personal financial statement.

> " What you watch will grow. What you measure, you can impact."

You may be asking yourself, "It seems like a lot of energy to put into this activity. How will I benefit?" The answer is simple: What you watch will grow. What you measure, you can impact. It's proven, and it will change the way you build your life and your wealth.

This process is ever-evolving. You may even acquire 30 entities in addition to your ME, Inc., like Paul. When you add up the cost of bookkeeping, accounting, and corporate compliance, it might make sense to have a chief financial officer and perhaps even a compliance officer in-house.

Our vision is for your corporation to grow to the point where it is a living, breathing entity that creates jobs and cash flow for you, your family, and your team. Eventually, it can even have a new CEO.

WEALTH ACCELERATOR

It's never too soon to begin your own ME, Inc. View your life and money flows from a corporate perspective, enhanced by people, systems, leverage, measured goals, and results.

CHAPTER 7

THE IMPORTANCE OF HAVING A "GROUND GAME" AND AN "AIR GAME"

There are some people who live in a dream world,
and there are some who face reality; and then there are
those who turn one into the other.
—Douglas H. Everett

The Way of Work

Implementing our concept of having a good "ground game" and a good "air game" will help you build wealth. It took David a while to learn this. When he got started in real estate, there were no office hours. He figured he could just work longer and have more wins. Sure enough, as he began to have success, he started working as many hours a day as he could. He even found a comrade-in-arms, a fellow realtor, Pat Hiban, and they started competing on the number of hours they worked each day. At the end of the week, they would email each other their total hours worked. Though David usually lost more than he won, he loved the energy of competing. But eventually working 14-hour days grew exhausting. It was fun being young, full of energy, and whipping the work. It was also completely mind numbing. Years went by like this until he got a wake-up call.

The Hazards of Grinding

One day while working insane hours, David got a painful rash on his chest. It hurt so much that he couldn't sleep. The doctor told him he had shingles. David was only 31 years old and his doctor said it was stress-related. David used this experience as an opportunity to reflect; and he's since come to appreciate that early wake-up call. Since that day, he made a shift and hired some coaches. One of them changed his perspective by telling him that he was like a serf. He was making a great income for a 31-year-old, but the way he treated himself was like an indentured servant. When he traveled, he stayed in cheap hotels and rented cheap cars. He created all that income for himself with no reward. He was just working to earn for some future day that was never likely to come.

A Balanced Attack

What David learned from this experience was that the way of wealth requires a balanced attack. You have to have a good ground game and a good air game.

> " You have to have a good ground game and a good air game."

Your "ground game" is getting to work, gutting it out, grinding away, and getting things done. If you are in sales, your ground game is making calls, getting appointments, and closing sales. If you are in construction, your ground game is getting the work, doing the job, building the home or plant, hiring the subs, and whatever else it takes to get the work completed. Lots of people have a solid ground game but no air game. Their earnings can range from very little (hourly employees) to quite a bit (professional athletes).

You know you have a ground game when you are earning a paycheck and doing a good job. If you are great at work, you have a good ground game. But a good ground game is not enough to build wealth. You also need to balance that with a good air game.

Far fewer people have a good air game, which includes your plan, strategy, and tactics. You must make a good plan and evaluate yourself against it, or you risk ending up like Alice in Wonderland, who had the following exchange with the Cheshire Cat when she was at a crossroads:[1]

> *"Would you tell me, please, which way I ought to go from here?" said Alice.*
>
> *"That depends a good deal on where you want to get to," said the Cat.*
>
> *"I don't much care where," said Alice.*
>
> *"Then it doesn't matter which way you go," said the Cat.*

Like Alice, if you don't have a plan for your life, the first person you meet will give you one. However, if you want ultimate influence over where you go, then create a vision for yourself. If you choose a direction, define your goals, and select a purpose that aligns with your talents and your passions, pretty soon your life will become more fulfilling. You will naturally attract people to your life who have a purpose, with passions that run along the same lines as yours. So, have a plan and develop a good air game. The best thing about the air game is it only takes one hour per week. If you give yourself just 1 hour per week, or 50 hours per year, you will blow by your previous best with very little effort. This is time very well spent; don't skip it.

It's important to have a balanced attack. For example, if you have

---

1   Lewis Carroll, *Alice's Adventures in Wonderland*, 1865.

a good air game but no ground game, you'll end up planning all the time without following through. Success requires both.

For example, a guy we know, let's call him Mike, works 70+ hours a week. Mike is 59. He has worked 70+ hours a week since he was a young man. It's what he does. What's interesting about Mike is that even though he has made millions from his work, he doesn't have much to show for it. You see, Mike has been so focused on his work that he hasn't created his air game. Mike is a grinder. He has an excellent ground game, making things happen through the sheer force of his actions. But he hasn't built wealth, because by focusing solely on his ground game, he has overlooked how he might leverage his significant talent.

At the other end of the spectrum, David once hired an Ivy League MBA to get into real estate sales. The employee dressed well, was extremely smart, and had great air game. But he had no ground game. He refused to grind it out, even a little bit. Six months later he put together an amazing listing presentation, but no one ever saw it. As a result, he was out of business in less than a year. His lack of ground game meant no results and no income.

WEALTH ACCELERATOR

You have to have a good air game (planning and vision skills) to take full advantage of your earnings skills. You also have to have a good ground game (grinding through your work and making things happen) to execute your plan. People tend to be naturally good at one or the other. What comes easily to you? Create an awareness that building wealth requires both.

CHAPTER 8

ASSET-BASED LIVING VERSUS CASH-FLOW-BASED LIVING

It's easy to come up with new ideas; the hard part is
letting go of what worked for you two years ago,
but will soon be out of date.
—Roger von Oech

Building wealth requires asset-based living. To demonstrate the difference between asset-based living and cash-flow-based living, let's look at two situations involving a lottery winner. Both win $1 million after taxes.

The first guy takes the $1 million over ten years at $100,000 a year in income. Maybe he gets a bump because of the future value of money, so he gets $120,000 a year over ten years. He has a great ten years. He lives well, buys a nice car and a nice house. He relaxes for ten years and doesn't work at all. Life is good—that is until the ten years are up. Then he has to sell the house and the car, because he cannot afford them anymore. He goes back to work, but at least he has a story to tell.

The second person takes the lump sum. She invests her $1 million dollars in real estate. She is fairly conservative and buys ten homes worth $150,000 each and only borrows $500,000. She rents them out for an average of $1,800 a month. That earns her a gross income of

$18,000 a month. Forty percent, or $7,200 a month, goes to repairs, taxes, and vacancy, leaving her with $10,800 a month. Further, she has to pay off the $500,000, which is at 5% interest on a 15-year note and costs her $4,000 a month. This includes principle pay down and leaves her $6,000 a month or $72,000 a year in net income. She lives well, but it is a fair amount less than the other lottery winner. However, she also makes an extra payment each year of $4,000, so she lives on approximately $5,500 extra a month or 60% of the first guy's revenue.

Unlike the first lottery winner, she doesn't quit her job and doesn't change her life other than developing some skills at managing her rental properties. She pays off the $500,000 in ten years. At the end of the same ten years she has ten homes that have now appreciated $50,000 each in value. Her net worth is now $2 million. Her passive income grew from modest rent increases and her debt is paid down to zero. She now has an extra $144,000 a year for the rest of her life, and she owns the assets, which continue to appreciate over time.

The first guy lived on his cash flow, while the woman practiced asset-based living. She lived off the income produced by her assets. Very few of us win the lottery; most people receive a paycheck twice a month. If you spend your life living off your paycheck, you're living off your cash flow. If instead you live below your means and save the extra cash, you can use that cash to buy assets. This will put you on the path of asset-based living. If you practice this discipline, you'll have cash flow from those assets. Eventually you'll be able to live off the income. This is the way the wealthy live, and it is possible for you!

WEALTH ACCELERATOR

The simplest way to build wealth is to live below your means and to invest your excess cash flow wisely. The sooner you save cash to invest, the sooner you learn how to invest it. One thing is for sure: Without building assets, you will almost certainly never become wealthy.

Wealth Comes in Waves

Be aware that wealth comes in waves. Suppose you add assets to your portfolio—smart assets, well-positioned assets. Rather than growing in a straight line, increasing your net worth 3% to 5% year after year, they may be flat for five years and then jump 50% in two years. Markets rise and fall in a jerky manner rather than exhibiting straight-line growth.

> " Buy assets that will survive most down markets with positive cash flow."

How do you take advantage of this truth? Accumulate well-positioned assets, purchased intelligently, that grow when the market jumps. How? Buy assets that will survive most down markets with positive cash flow. Accumulate as many of these intelligent assets as possible, and then when the market jumps, you will reap an unfair share of the market rise.

We both use basic investing disciplines and realize that neither of us can perfectly time the market. We buy smart assets in any market. Without attempting to time the markets, we kept building our portfolios, adding lots of real estate assets well before and during the downturn of 2008–2011. Then, when the market started rising in 2012 and 2013, we gained more in terms of net asset value, or net worth, than at any other time in our lives. We had spent nearly two decades living below our means and picking up smart assets. And when the markets jumped, our net worth jumped with them.

We define smart assets as those assets that are either purchased below market value or need modest improvements that add value, and that are purchased with smart debt or no debt. Debt is "smart debt" when your total cash flow is greater with the debt than it would be without the debt. And, when you still have a cushion in case the asset goes down in value. You have this when your cash flow covers debt even in a market downturn.

The Asset-Based Life and the Cash-Flow Life—Which One Are You Living?

Let's be clear: Very few people live off the money produced by their assets. Recently, we looked at the income of the top 1% of the United States. The range varies depending on what part of the country you live in. We were shocked that you needed to earn only $384,000 in Charlotte, North Carolina, and $608,000 in New York City to be in that elite of elite groups. But, how many of those folks have enough income-producing assets to fund 100% of their expenses? We would be surprised if more than 1% of the top 1% were doing so.

How do you move from a cash-flow-based life to an asset-based life without feeling too much of a financial pinch? The first step is to measure separately your income flow from work and your income flow from assets. Then, create a "Dream Budget." Finally, match your income sources to your current budget and your Dream Budget. And, plan for a future where your income flow from your cash-flowing assets covers your budget.

We have spent decades building assets, and we have finally reached a point where our passive income is several times greater than our living expenses. The first—and in some ways most important—step is to measure income and expenses and perform a gap analysis. We suggest taking income and separating it into two types. The first is money in exchange for work, or regular income. The second is money that comes from assets or "passive income." When we first did this analysis, there was a huge gap. It's useful to do this even if you have zero income-producing assets—you can still measure the gap. To begin to address this gap, we started with a simple strategy: We always made sure that we earned a little bit more than we needed to live on, and we never outspent what we earned.

> ❝ We always made sure that we earned a little bit more than we needed to live on, and we never outspent what we earned."

Another step we took included putting tax-deferred money into our retirement accounts every year. It's a good plan, but it's just the beginning. Living within your means is a great start to wealth building. Next, we both chose to build assets and wealth. We began building wealth by investing money in something we knew fairly well—real estate, using money invested by friends and family. This is called "syndication," and it's one of the fastest ways to build assets.

WEALTH ACCELERATOR

First, always max out on your tax-deferred investments. It is a great path, but it's only the beginning path to asset-based living. Next, implement one or more of the fastest ways to build income-producing assets: use other people's money (often referred to as "OPM"), take a job that pays in salary and equity, and build a business and get investors.

Real estate is an excellent investment vehicle and lends itself well to using other people's money. That's because everyone—with some tutoring—can evaluate a real estate investment and make good choices.

Build Income-Producing Equity to Achieve Asset-Based Living

Some real estate deals begin the same way. They are called "development deals." They can look like this: Here is empty land. Let's buy it, develop it, and hope they (tenants) will come. Even in this, the far-riskier type of real estate deal—you can pre-rent to tenants. In fact, most developers have their tenants ready to go before they begin spending money on a deal. Compared to a restaurant deal, it's almost like cheating. Can you imagine starting a restaurant and preselling 80% of your pizza at a set price, locked in for ten years?

So, how did we sell investors on our real estate concept? It wasn't very hard. We showed them an actual property. We showed them the actual income and expenses. And we showed them the actual current return. Then, we presented a predictable strategy to increase income and reduce expenses over time, which increases profit, return, and the value of the investment. Further, because you can readily get bank loans for real estate (if you put down 30%, you can get money in any market), you can create leverage to increase your return on capital using investors' capital as part or all of the down payment, plus the bank's money.

This is the path that we've been using for decades to create wealth. After a long while of building equity or wealth, we realized that we still were not generating enough income to fund our lives. We were moving toward our wealth goals but not our passive-income goals. We first saw this clearly when we began to break our personal financial statements and income statements into income from active and passive sources.

By doing this, we could see income from active sources increasing (working harder, working smarter, expanding our consulting work). We could also see our net worth growing as our real estate assets grew larger every year with appreciation (even just the rise of inflation) coupled with leverage and paying down the mortgage (owing less on the same property) every single month. But, the actual cash stream from passive income was not growing fast enough to both pay off investors and keep up with our increasing spending.

At that point, perhaps seven years ago, we decided to laser focus on building assets that would create cash flow. We worked harder in the areas where we earned money and equity and positioned ourselves better. And we began buying real estate—cash-flow-focused real estate—with our own money.

The combination of those forces has brought us to the place where we finally earn more money from our passive-income-producing assets than our income from our work. And, that passive income alone now well outpaces our living expenses. If we stopped working today, our active income would go to zero. But our passive income would cover all our expenses without disrupting our lifestyle or investment strategies.

WEALTH ACCELERATOR

Create awareness. Make sure you have a personal financial statement that you keep up to date. This is simply a list of all your assets, your debts (liabilities), and the total, giving you your net worth. Then create a Profit & Loss (P&L) or income statement. This is a list of all your income—broken into two categories: income coming from passive sources and income coming from your work or active sources. This P&L statement should also list all of your expenses.

Assets Let You Take Advantage of Downturns

The reality of downturns is that they often help the wealthy get wealthier. In fact, the number of millionaires hit an all-time high in 2013, just a few years after the Great Recession. Why is that? Why do the wealthy thrive after a downturn?

The reason is simple. Even though a downturn hurts the wealthy—the number of millionaires dropped in 2008 and 2009—they still have enough cash to buy assets when the price of assets has dropped dramatically. And if you keep buying, you're going to massively increase your wealth as the economy recovers. In 2008 and 2009, asset prices, especially real estate, plummeted 30–40% and sometimes even more. The government began a policy of keeping interest rates very low to help kick-start the economy. This did nothing for a while, as there was widespread panic. But eventually it began to inflate asset prices.

When you buy a home, it's not the price of the home that matters, unless you are paying all cash. What matters is the combination of price and interest rate. In reality, you are buying a payment. So, when rates are low, you can buy more house, or buy the identically priced house for less cash outlay per month. Slowly, as prices and interest rates combined to make housing very affordable, people began to buy again. By 2016 residential real estate was red hot. Prices were going up fast, and anyone who bought anything in 2010 through 2012 did great. Who is most likely to have bought something at the bottom of the market? To buy something at the bottom, you had to have some cash and great credit. Who is likely to have those two things? Wealthy people. So, their wealth went up if they added assets when the market hit bottom.

Because we are both in real estate, it became more and more obvious between 2009 and 2011 that real estate was at a bottom. We saw that there was going to be a rise in the value of real estate. And we weren't the only ones. A herd of investors saw the same opportunity, and that herd lifted real estate out of the depths it was in and created a boom that occurred in 2013. Both of us invested heavily during this window. And because of it, 2012 and 2013 were some of their best years ever for building wealth.

Andy Beal of Beal Bank was sitting around playing cards during the last boom. He had a high cash-to-assets ratio, and the FDIC was bugging him to loan out some of that cash. The reality was that he saw everything as too hot in 2001 through 2007, so he was sitting it out on the sidelines, playing bridge every day and not investing. When the market crashed, he went all in, buying tons of assets at pennies on the dollar. In 2016 his net worth was estimated at $9 billion. Today he's probably sitting on all that cash again.

So how do you take advantage of this type of downturn? The first thing to do is commit 100% to whatever sector you're in. That is, don't spend time chasing multiple rabbits. Instead, stay focused. Over time you will develop awareness and expertise. And when you develop these skills, you will recognize a good time to throw down in your sector. This is how you begin to discern the cycles of your sector.

WEALTH ACCELERATOR

Generally, business cycles last approximately seven years. To navigate these cycles to your advantage, start accumulating cash when things seem hot. When things drop precipitously, wait a little bit for the dust to clear and then build your assets at significant discounts. Crashes are always more violent and quicker than booms. Thus, prices get more severely discounted more quickly when things go south. If you are familiar with the cycle and become an expert in your sector, opportunities will materialize.

Horizontal and Vertical Income

Ralph Waldo Emerson said, "The mind, once stretched by a new idea, never returns to its original dimensions." The concept that we are about to share with you will not only stretch your mind, it will also grow your business.

David's friend Tim Rhode told him shortly after he met him that he had 18 paychecks a month coming in. "Eighteen paychecks a month!" he said. "How is that possible?" David asked. "Simple," Tim said. "I have eighteen investments that send me a check every month."

Since then, David has never thought of his investments in any way other than paychecks. Why have only one paycheck? He now spends a lot of his time seeking out what we call horizontal income. Today, he is up to about 30+ monthly paychecks.

Expand the part of your brain that sees income only as a vertical (money earned through work) option. We all have the opportunity to receive multiple streams of horizontal income. Eventually, most people will have income from social security, maybe a work pension, some potential interest income from fixed income, some dividends from your 401(k), and finally any rental income from any rental properties you own. If you get this key point—that your financial future will be horizontal income—then why not build a plan today to expand your horizontal income streams?

Vertical (Earned) versus Horizontal (Passive) Income

The concept of vertical income is something we're taught in school: Develop a skill or trade, take it to the marketplace, and earn income.

The income you earn hopefully goes up over time as you get better at your craft. Vertical income comes naturally to us. Everyone does it.

VERTICAL INCOME
What You Do To Make Money

Figure 8.1

Horizontal income, by contrast, is all of your income that comes from investment sources. Most people only have vertical income. Developing horizontal income is not taught. It's a skill that you must develop. It's a key pillar of your financial freedom plan and a gauge of your progress in asset-based living.

Start thinking of vertical income as a tool to create horizontal income, where vertical income minus expenses equals money left over to invest. When you learn to invest your money wisely, you begin to change your financial future. And, instead of thinking about how to get a 5% raise at your job (vertical income), you build a financial plan that creates true and lasting financial freedom.

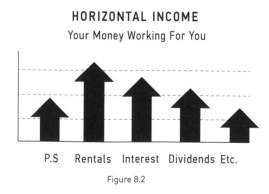

HORIZONTAL INCOME
Your Money Working For You

Figure 8.2

How Much Horizontal Income Is Enough?

The answer is simple: whatever it takes to fund your lifestyle. It should include money for investing, saving, and contribution. In other words, the answer is not driven by money but rather by how much is necessary to be able to do what you want, when you want.

Bear the following tips in mind when creating horizontal income:

- Be patient. Build your portfolio slowly.
- Leverage (financial debt) when it makes sense, but don't over-leverage (creating excessive risk).
- Be a "100% er," that is, aim to have 100% of your expenses covered by your horizontal income streams.
- Don't let the market take you down. Have enough equity in the property and enough free cash flow to make sure all bills can be paid and thus be safe in a declining market.
- Spend less and earn more. Be careful not to increase spending equal to your income increase.
- Shift your thinking from working for money to working for wealth.
- Shift your thinking from gross income or bonus to net income and money left to invest.
- Create a vision, a plan, a goal, and a peer group to hold you accountable.
- Become aware of, and open to, opportunities.
- If you're cash poor, look for partners and combine resources. And, if possible, do it in a way so you can lead the opportunity.
- $1 of passive income equals $10 of earned income.

WEALTH ACCELERATOR

Don't wait until retirement to think about your horizontal income and multiple passive-income streams. Start today by focusing on how you can build multiple streams of income that will serve you for a lifetime!

" Shift your thinking from working for money to working for wealth."

BONUS CONTENT:
WAVES OF INCOME

Wealth comes in waves, and you can either ride the wave or get submerged by it. Our online bonus for this chapter uses three scenarios to give you the insight you need to successfully ride the wealth waves. Access it now by going to www.wealthcantwait.com/waves.

CHAPTER 9

MAKING IT HAPPEN WITH EASE

What we really want to do is what we are really
meant to do. When we do what we are meant to do,
money comes to us, doors open for us, we feel useful,
and the work we do feels like play to us.
—Julia Cameron

What Do You Want in Your Life?

Building wealth can happen with ease. First, let's distinguish *ease* from *easy*. To us, living a life of ease is pursuing the things we want in life. Contrast that with doing what others want us to do or what we perceive we should be doing, and we experience the path without ease. The path toward ease is not the path of least resistance—it is a path of varying resistances—but it is the path toward what you want in your life.

WEALTH ACCELERATOR

Ask yourself, "What do I want in my life?"

Here's our answer: love, connection, family, abundance, growth, sex, wealth, health, vitality, leadership impact, creating a legacy, and, yes, ease.

If you are like us, you would want to ask the same question over and over again, being mindful of doing so while having no judgment. Forget about what others want you to have in your life or what you think you should have in your life. Do this for yourself, and keep in mind that we can be our own harshest critics.

WEALTH ACCELERATOR

Ask yourself again, "What do I want in my life?" And this time, ask the question with zero judgment.

With Ease

We are programmed to believe that what we want in our lives, if it has any value at all, should come at a tremendous cost, be it time, effort, money, or sacrifice. That belief stands in the way of living as big a life as we are capable of living. For example, Paul wants a net worth of $100 million—not because it's a random large number, but because he knows what it would bring into his life: freedom—the power to choose and create.

Why wouldn't you want $100 million in net worth? Well, without winning the lotto, it seems like it would require too much sacrifice, taking away from other vital things like time with your family. But, here is an epiphany: Who says that journey must include massive personal sacrifice? What if you could have everything you want in your life and have ease?

Somewhere we got brainwashed that what we truly want can't come with ease. But that's just not true. Ask for it. Seek it. And strive for it while you seek and reach for your goals.

> " If you get stuck, start dreaming."

And if you get stuck, start dreaming. Paul likes to imagine what he would do if he won the lottery. For example, he might create the entrepreneurial foundation that he has been dreaming about for a decade. One that truly feeds his soul (working with other talented people in a creative, lively workspace), plays to his unique abilities (providing vision and energy to a project), and has systems (staff and workarounds) for the parts of work he either does not enjoy or where he is lacking.

Pondering hypotheticals like these gives us a window into how we would like our lives to be. It is practical and logical. Without the $100 million, we may not have the resources to implement the entire picture, but at least we know where we're headed and what to shoot for. And that is a valuable lesson in creating ease.

WEALTH ACCELERATOR

How would you create your life if money were not an obstacle? What would you be willing to receive? What would you love to do? What would bring you true fulfillment? What would you do if you won the lotto and netted $100 million?

Your Magic Zone Is Where Passion Meets Ability

Now we're going to get into the zone, and we're going to use Paul to get there. Paul would really, really love to be an NBA star. He is passionate about the game, but he doesn't have the talent, youth, or physicality to succeed at this goal. It just isn't going to happen. That dose of reality is what prevents a fool's errand in a world where the self-help gurus teach us to "Think Big."

Paul's childhood friend Alan Paul, one of the few guys who loved basketball even more than he did as a kid but had even less ability, found his magic zone, the place where his passion met his ability. Al's true passions are basketball and music, specifically guitar.

He graduated with a degree in journalism from the University of Michigan. Unlike his wife, Rebecca, now Managing Editor of *The Wall Street Journal*, Al was not an ace journalism student. But he was a guy who quietly and in his own way relentlessly pursued his passions. At various points in the last ten years, Al was Managing Editor of *Slam* Magazine and *Guitar World*. He flew on private jets interviewing NBA stars, sat courtside for big games, and is very close friends with legendary guitarist Gregg Allman of the Allman Brothers. Al recently wrote *One Way Out: The Inside History of the Allman Brothers Band.*

Ever open to possibility, Al encouraged his wife to take the post of chief of The Wall Street Journal's China Bureau during the Olympics in Beijing. He had to play Mr. Mom as they dragged their three young children around the globe. He walked away from his work to do this.

While in China, he met some great Chinese musicians who shared his love of the blues. They formed a blues band—which no doubt would have struggled in the US—but was a big hit in China. Before his China adventure was over, Al was headlining music festivals across China. You can read about this amazing adventure in his book *Big in China.*

Likewise, Paul's buddy Dan Segal combined his law degree (and disdain for the practice of law) with his lifelong love of soccer to open what is now the largest US Soccer representation firm. Was this the path of least resistance? Not by a long shot. It took Dan a decade (after leaving his high-paying law firm job) to make a decent living at it. After years of hard-core battle, he chose to swallow his pride and partner with his top competitor to form the firm with the largest market share. That move made them a viable candidate for acquisition by the ever-growing powerhouse Wasserman Media Group.

Ease Is Different from the Path of Least Resistance

If you continually assess what you want in your life and move toward those choices, then you are choosing a life of ease. Having what you want creates ease. It does not mean that the path is easy or that it is the path of least resistance. Often the opposite can happen. Going for what is "easy" can take us away from ease by taking us off course and not pursuing the things we love. For example, the prospect of a high-paying job can lure us away from the grind of building our own business.

> " Having what you want creates ease."

Creating harmony in a meaningful relationship is another way we create ease. We all enjoy the parts of relationships that work for us, but at some point, we have to confront the parts that aren't working. Let's say your partner does something unintentionally that steps onto one of your childhood wounds. The path of least resistance would be to just to let it go while resentment and anger build inside you. Having the tough conversation right away is not pleasant or easy, yet confronting it leads to ease. Creating healthy boundaries with a partner or child or coworker is a great example of something that creates a lifetime of ease but isn't necessarily easy.

You Fight Ease When You Focus on the Negative

What we focus on expands. Focus on problems and challenges, and guess what? You'll get more of them. Paul remembers a NASCAR driver who was being interviewed. The driver was asked about what he did in the split second when cars started to crash all around him. His answer was to drive the car to where the crashing, careening cars weren't. At first, that seemed like an odd answer. But the more he thought about it, the more he saw genius in that answer. Your vehicle, like it or not, tends to go toward what you focus on. That's the metaphor, and it's a powerful one for our lives.

" Do you focus on the crash or the opportunity?"

Do you focus on the crash or the opportunity? Like the NASCAR driver, if you focus on the opportunity and make it through the "crash," there are fewer cars competing, and your odds of winning go up. What you focus on, you naturally put energy into. Wouldn't it be better to focus on the opportunity instead of the crash?

Every time you bump into adversity, ask yourself this question: "What is the opportunity in this for me?" There is an opportunity to grow and learn in almost any situation. Using the NASCAR driver as a metaphor, "What would your life look like if you chose to focus on the path of opportunities rather than the crashing cars?"

Choosing *ease* is not choosing *easy*. And we're not suggesting that you ignore the cars crashing in front of and around you. Driving blindly won't help your cause. Instead, we're saying notice and learn from, but don't focus on, the crash. Focus on the opportunity that lies within every situation that you encounter in your life. It's hard to do. Few of us do it naturally. But in those tough instances lie your greatest opportunities.

WEALTH ACCELERATOR

There is ease in every path. When on a path that is true to you, work becomes easy. "Hard" things aren't hard when they lie on your path to becoming who you truly are.

CHAPTER 10

TAKING RESPONSIBILITY FOR YOUR WEALTH

Let others lead small lives, but not you. Let others argue over small things, but not you. Let others cry over small hurts, but not you. Let others leave their future in someone else's hands, but not you. And remember the four things that never return: the spoken word, the speeding arrow, the wasted life, and the neglected opportunity.
—Dennis Kimbro

Building wealth begins with taking responsibility for your wealth. Paul's first brush with wealth was interacting with his dad's first cousin, Charles. Paul's cousin died more than 30 years ago with more than $100 million in net worth, which would be closer to $220 million today. Charles did not receive a formal education. His parents gave him zero dollars. And he didn't hit the lotto or get lucky in any way.

> " Building wealth begins with taking responsibility for your wealth."

Charles was the first person Paul had ever met who could do exactly what he wanted to do, when he wanted to do it. Paul noticed that one thing that set Charles apart from everyone else—he did not complain and he did not blame. If you stop and try to find one person in your life who does not complain and does not blame, you will be hard-pressed.

WEALTH ACCELERATOR

The most important Accelerator for wealth building might also be the most important Accelerator for life, and that is: Take responsibility for *everything* in your life—good and bad.

One thing we know is that having a no-excuse habit is the single greatest change you can make in your life. That one change makes you the creator of your own reality. We don't mean that in a way that is inconsistent with a Higher Power or any religion. Your God, whether Judeo-Christian, Eastern, Muslim, or any other, does not want you to play small.

At this point in your life, we don't believe there's one single excuse for not being where you want to be. It is all on your shoulders. And though that is scary sometimes and can be hard in the moment, you become empowered as soon as you stop making excuses for the events in your life. That is the ultimate wealth truth.

Right now, despite your education level, despite your family history, despite your level of intelligence, despite anything, you have the power to reach your wealth goals. As soon as you believe that, you are ready to accept what you deserve.

Here's the question Paul always asks: "What do I want in life?" That question is relatively easy to understand. Here's a seemingly more complicated question: "What am I willing to receive?" The answer to that question is tied to how much responsibility you take for where you are in your life. It doesn't matter if you're flat broke or well on your way to building the wealth you want.

Accept this truth: You're exactly where you are because of your actions and who you are "being," how you are showing up in the world. As soon as you accept that, you're willing to receive.

Take Responsibility for Everything

This shift, if you can make it, will change everything. It will change your personal world, your business world, and all your relationships. Plain and simple, if you are involved, you have some level of control. And, if it does not go well, it's on you. Listen to that statement. Internalize it, accept it, and surrender to it.

Let's demonstrate this another way by looking at extremes. If you don't take responsibility for anything, you are a tiny ball in the world's pinball machine. You get blasted from one bumper to the next. None of it is in your control. Conversely, if you choose to take responsibility for everything—your past, your present, and your future—suddenly you are 100% in control.

People don't like all of life's outcomes and so they shy away from responsibility. It's natural to take credit (as we should) when something goes right, but then take no responsibility when it does not go well. "You reap what you sow" is one of the best lessons in life. If you thought about it before every interaction you had with another person, your life would work for you.

Here's one more benefit of taking responsibility: You can begin or perpetuate a virtuous cycle. When you're willing to take responsibility, your willingness creates space for those around you to take responsibility. Consider the opposite: Nothing makes another person more defensive than blaming them for a bad outcome.

WEALTH ACCELERATOR

Taking responsibility for everything has a positive effect on those around you.

The Power of Choice

Don't underestimate the power of words and the emotions they create. When you "have to" or "need to" do something, it carries a heaviness along with it that saps your energy. It is as if there is an outside force requiring it. It seems real, but is it?

For instance, look at the statement "I have to go to work." Do you really have to? We have a friend, not a wealthy man, who just decided not to go to work anymore. Instead, he collects disability and child support and fritters away his time. He hasn't worked a day in ten years. We may not choose this path, but it is certainly an option.

Think about the statement "I have to pay my mortgage." Do you really have to? We knew someone who was living in a gorgeous house worth millions of dollars. Times got tough, and he didn't make a mortgage payment in over three years. Eventually, he worked it out with the debtor who bought the note from the bank. This guy used every tool possible to stay in the house. If you really looked at it, you would be surprised by what you really have to do versus what you choose to do.

The same goes for your kids. Do they ever ask you to not go in to work and stay home with them instead? Chances are you tell them you have to go to work. Think about that for a second. Do you really have to go? Not really, but you choose to go. The next time your kids ask you to stay home, think about their proposal. If you truly want to go to work, let them know that. You can explain that it pays the bills, but that it's still your choice. And then offer an alternative way to spend time with them. Or, if you truly don't need to go in that day, then take the day off. In the grand scheme of things, which choice will have a bigger impact on your life?

Consider the possibility of removing "have to" and "need to" from your vocabulary—except when you are referring to a trip to the bathroom. Very few things in life are not a choice. Instead, choose empowering language. That language, in turn, will shape the way you think. And that will lead you on the path to ease.

" Consider the possibility of removing 'have to' and 'need to' from your vocabulary."

BONUS CONTENT:
TAKE RESPONSIBILITY

The bonus for this chapter consists of two powerful stories. The first illustrates taking responsibility, even when someone wrongs you. The second demonstrates the importance of putting away excuses and learning from those who have built wealth.

You can access them at www.wealthcantwait.com/Responsibility.

CHAPTER 11

DEALING WITH SETBACKS

It's not the situation, but whether we react (negative) or
respond (positive) to the situation that's important.
—Zig Ziglar

To build wealth with ease, consider your emotional reaction to setbacks. As you steadfastly pursue wealth building, eventually you will hit a roadblock. It's simply a part of the process. A full life always has its measure of setbacks.

Here are two ways you can turn the tables on any setback:

- First, know that you control every outcome. Consider the following formula: Event + Response = Outcome, or E + R = O.
- Second, know that if you are willing to win, you can. If you look hard enough, you can find advantages in every setback.

Event + Response = Outcome

Events can be one of three things: neutral, positive, or negative. Let's look at what would widely be perceived as a tragic/negative event. Say you got fired, crashed your car, were diagnosed with cancer, your partner had a miscarriage, or your son was murdered. Life deals out its fair share of tragedy. No one, no matter how wealthy, is immune from such horrible events.

Let's explore the formula in more detail. The event—regardless of what it is—happened in the past. But your response to that event will affect the outcome. That's the beauty of E + R = O. Dr. Wayne Dyer uses a metaphor of how the things that happen to us are like the giant wake behind a speeding boat. We see this massive wake—it's visible and it's powerful. But as humans, we make the mistake of thinking that the wake powers the boat. It doesn't. The engine and the rudder, connected to the steering wheel that we control, steer the boat and guide our path into the future. Dr. Dyer doesn't advocate ignoring the wake. Instead, acknowledge it for what it is: It is in the past. And it does not determine where the boat goes in the future. We are in control of that.

" Events have the meaning that we give to them."

Events have the meaning that we give to them. Let's demonstrate this by showing you how the same event—in different contexts—creates very different outcomes. Remember we have the power to create. The most powerful part of an outcome is the meaning that we give to something.

There is an old proverb about a Taoist farmer that goes something like this: A boy falls off a horse and fractures his leg. The family says: "Oh no! How horrible!" The wise man says: "You can't be sure it's horrible." Then the army comes and conscripts all able-bodied boys. They leave the boy at home because of the bad fracture. The family says: "Wow, you were right. It's a blessing the boy fractured his leg." The wise man says: "You can't be sure it's a blessing." Then famine strikes the village, and the boys who were conscripted were at least well fed and cared for and had a greater chance of survival. The family says:

"Oh, how horrible! If he hadn't fractured his leg, he would have been well fed."

The point to the proverb is this: You just don't know what outcome will result from an event in your life. But with E + R = O, you can do a lot to affect that outcome.

WEALTH ACCELERATOR

Are you willing to win under any circumstance? If so, we challenge you to face any adversity, from mild to severe, and ask yourself: "What about this event could benefit me? What happened that could be to my advantage?" The answer might not be obvious, but if you ask this over and over—and you are open to the answer—you'll find one. This is because there is something positive for you, something to your advantage, inside *any* negative event.

A chiropractor we know has a nephew named Jesse, who was an amazing athlete on his way to becoming a pro surfer when disaster struck. Jesse was surfing and broke a vertebra in his neck and severed his spinal cord, leaving him a quadriplegic.

Jesse found advantages in his setback and put E + R = O to work for him. He is now back to surfing, leading an amazing life. He founded the Life Rolls On foundation and was featured in the film *Into the Liquid*. He was also given a lifetime surfing achievement award, received the prestigious Nike Casey Martin Award, and is a highly sought-after motivational speaker. What can you learn from Jesse? How will you apply E + R = O to your life the next time "tragedy" strikes?

PART

EMBRACE THE MINDSET
THAT BUILDS WEALTH

TWO

CHAPTER 12

THINK—THEN GROW RICH

It is far easier to build wealth if you expect to be wealthy.
—Great Uncle Ted

So much of wealth is about who you are and how you see the world. Wealth is about mindset, expectation, and mental commitment. As Felix Dennis says in *The Narrow Road,* "Getting rich comes from an attitude of mind."

David considers himself lucky in a way. His grandmother was a poor child from a wealthy family. His great uncle in England let them live on his estate in Surrey while David's dad was serving in the army. David's family stayed in an extra house that would've been the groundskeeper's house. While he was at boarding school in Surrey, David's parents would stay there. The relative he was most often around as a young man was Uncle Ted, who was a multimillionaire back in 1975.

David worked on his uncle's farm. His uncle was a hard worker and taught David the value of hard work from an early age. He also taught him the importance of mindset. David will never forget what he said to him one day, "It's far easier to build wealth if you expect to be wealthy." And having built considerable wealth, we can tell that it's true—when you look at the world in the right way, and approach it in the right way, the right things tend to happen. And it all starts with your attitude and expectation.

It's Far Easier to Build Wealth When You're Around the Wealthy

It's no surprise to us that Warren Buffett donated his money to the Gates Foundation. It's also no surprise to us that Warren and Bill are friends, or that they play bridge together. Wealth attracts wealth just as poverty attracts poverty. If you're surrounded by poverty and raised in poverty, the odds of being poor are increased dramatically. No government program is likely to change this, because wealth and poverty are primarily mindsets. Wealthy people have a mindset that's contagious. Poor people have a mindset that's contagious. So, if you want to build wealth, hang out with, learn from, and attract a community that supports wealth.

> " Wealthy people have a mindset that's contagious."

It's Far Easier to Build Wealth When You Think Correctly about Money

Consider the expression, "Money isn't everything." While correct, this thinking is exactly what those who do not have money say to keep themselves poor and possibly satisfied with a lack of wealth. Conversely, if you start thinking about money differently, your experience with it will change. Perhaps the best-known wealth book of all time is Napoleon Hill's *Think and Grow Rich*. If you haven't read it, we strongly recommend it. We also encourage you to think about the following:

- What role do you believe your thoughts play in building wealth?
- What is your position on money?
- What would you do with more financial abundance? Would it bring you closer to your destiny?
- What do you "know" about money?

Consider that last question. What do you know about wealth? Because if you don't come from an abundant perspective, building wealth will not follow. For instance, do you "know"—

- Money isn't everything?
- Money is the root of all evil?
- It takes money to make money?
- Most rich people are crooks?

Our perspective, or what we "know" about money, is at the heart of whether we live an abundant life or struggle with money. It's important to explore your beliefs about money and where you got them.

Learning an abundant mindset is at the heart of building wealth. And for many of us "unlearning" is just as important. Are you willing to unlearn the ideas that keep you exactly where you are? Choose wealth, choose abundance, and do not let any doubt creep between you and that destiny.

WEALTH ACCELERATOR

If you're willing to learn and unlearn, to choose to be that which you seek, to be wealth, and to do those things that lead to wealth, then nothing will stop you from achieving your goal of building wealth.

CHAPTER 13

THINK, "WHAT DO I WANT IN MY LIFE?"

While we try to teach our children all about life,
our children teach us what life is all about.
—Angela Schwindt

From Dreaming Big to Playing It Safe—and Back Again

How do you think big? For the best answers, ask a child. A child's thinking is limitless, free from what we learn is not possible. Life's "truths" can strip us of our childhood wonder and over time, we "unlearn" how to think big.

Just yesterday Paul's daughter asked him, "Why is the sky blue?" Paul was a little bummed that without Google, he didn't have an answer. Then, he was even more disappointed when he Googled it and read NASA's extremely complex explanation.

We're about to tell you something that could make you uncomfortable, but you need to hear it: Your grown-up "comfort zone" and your perception of reality is killing your dreams. The confines of your current reality stand in the way of all that you want to create. But there's a way back, and it starts with these powerful and expansive questions: If you could have anything your heart desired, what would that be? If you had no limits on your life, how would you live?

> **"** **If you could have anything your heart desired, what would that be? If you had no limits on your life, how would you live?"**

As a lawyer grinding away in a major New York law firm, Paul could not allow himself to dream of having business and personal freedom, creating a life of his design that included living in a house in the Santa Monica hills overlooking the ocean. It's sad to say, but lawyers, even successful partners at big law firms, most often cannot afford the $5 million required for such a purchase. And even if they could afford it, they certainly would not have the time to enjoy it. Why would Paul aspire to own that house or have other big dreams if he saw no possible path to having that and more in life?

This learned helplessness and hopelessness—based on "reality"—kills our dreams. So many people set their goals low, because they don't want to fail and they can't see possibility beyond the reaches of their current context. So, they "dumb down" what they want in life to match what they think they can accomplish, rather than what they would really like to have if they saw a path to achieving it.

Don't settle or dumb down. Instead, dream big. Let your imagination run wild. Identify and get in touch with what you really want in life. Suppose, for example, that you chose the amazing and important career as a public school teacher (this analysis works for any profession). The context of your current "reality" can be your "jail" or confinement of your aspirations if you allow that. Let's say you're currently earning $50,000 a year, including benefits. As you look into the future, what's possible for you? If you get your master's degree and have ten years on the job, you could earn $80,000 a year. If that salary funds your life's dreams, we would never suggest something different.

But, if you're reading this book, you probably want more than that. And, if you do want more, you must first relearn what you knew as a child: Think big and dream big.

> **❝ Think big and dream big."**

WEALTH ACCELERATOR

A basic, yet powerful and expansive way to think big is just to ask this simple question: "What do I want in my life?"

From Aspirations to Accomplishments

OK, now what? How do we turn our aspirations into reality? The first step is to see if the constructs of "What is" and "What was" stand in our way. Here are two examples to illustrate this. Let's say you want to be the CEO of a major corporation, perhaps like the one you're currently part of. Or you are a busboy at a posh restaurant, and you dream about owning the restaurant. Based on your current "reality," that might seem impossible. It's easy to look around, assess your current situation (what seems at first blush to be reality), and give up on your dream. But this reality is only a moment in time.

Some folks are stuck in the past. Do you know of a professional athlete, someone who used to be in the public spotlight, or even a friend who seems to have peaked early? Sometimes people are stuck with a notion of past greatness or what was, and that "reality" stops them from seeing themselves outside that "box" and in the future they want to create.

How many pro basketball players fade into nothing, retiring in their early thirties, and never accomplish much after? What about Bill Bradley—a basketball star both in high school and at Princeton.

Bradley won a gold medal in the Olympics, took two years off to attend graduate school, then had a successful ten-year run as an all-star NBA player who won two championships. His greatest accomplishments, however, came after basketball. He was a United States Senator and ran for President of the United States. He is a great example of how to live in the present and future without being tethered by the past.

WEALTH ACCELERATOR

See yourself as the future self you want to be.

The first step to accomplishing your dreams is to identify what you want your life to look like and what you want in your life. The second step is to create that future vision as if you're living it now, rather than just an outsider watching it. Putting yourself in your aspired reality and living it is what creates the change. If you want to create the impact, be the change you want in your life now. See yourself in that future life today.

> Putting yourself in your aspired reality and living it is what creates the change."

WEALTH ACCELERATOR

Be the change you want in your life. Today.

In addition to seeing things as they are (assessing your current reality), start seeing them as you would like them to be (assessing the possibility). Your mind is a very powerful, creative tool. And you access its power (for better or worse) through quality questions.

Whatever question you pose—your brain will begin to create the answer. Here's a familiar and painful example: Suppose that after you make an annoying mistake like forgetting to get to the parking meter in time, you ask yourself: "What the hell is wrong with me?" This question sets your brain in motion to search for and find an answer to that destructive question. If you ask the question enough times, you will create an answer that becomes your reality. Instead, ask yourself, "What could I be doing right now that would take me closer to achieving my aspirations?" If you ask this question over and over, your brain will find an answer.

BONUS CONTENT: WHAT DO YOU WANT IN LIFE?

We access—and unleash—the power of our minds through questions. We've prepared a special exercise to help you get in touch with what you want. You can access it at www.wealthcantwait.com/bonusXX.

CHAPTER 14

THINK, "I AM"

The more you see yourself as what you'd like to become,
and act as if what you want is already there, the more
you'll activate those dormant forces that will collaborate to
transform your dream into your reality.
—Wayne W. Dyer

There is a world of difference between thinking and saying "I can" or "I will" (which lack power), and thinking or saying "I am," "I have," or "It is" (which are very powerful). Therefore, it is important to choose your thoughts and words wisely.

"I am" is the most powerful phrase in our language. Dr. Wayne Dyer says you can redefine your self-concept by choosing which words to use after "I am." Like most things, this power cuts both ways. Add the word "not" to the sentence, and it can be devastating, as in the following examples:

- I am worthy. I am *not* worthy.
- I am capable. I am *not* capable.

For example, when speaking to a child it is critical to avoid saying things like "You are bad," "You are a brat," or, "You are impatient."

Instead say, "You are being a brat" or "You are being impatient." The former affects a child's self-concept, but when you insert "being" you are referring to present-tense behavior rather than an immutable character. Likewise, this is true for adults. Removing negative self-talk or modifying how you address others will have a huge impact.

Remaining positive doesn't mean you can't hold yourself or others accountable. For example, if you miss a deadline, say, "Darn it, I am better than that," "This is beneath my standards," or "I will do better next time." And when creating boundaries with others or correcting problem behaviors, try saying things like, "I would like for you to work on your patience," or "Your behavior is not acceptable to me. It is not OK to throw a Tonka truck at your brother."

WEALTH ACCELERATOR

We all make mistakes—whether large (like missing an important deadline) or small (like forgetting to put more money in a parking meter). Instead of reacting by using negative self-talk, replace it with positive, yet accountable, talk.

Affirm and Visualize

❝ To increase the power of your affirmations, add action words and emotional words that resonate deep inside you."

To create powerful affirmations, use the present tense, not the future. Use "I am" rather than "I will" or "I can." To increase the power of your affirmations, add action words and emotional words that resonate deep inside you. For instance: *I am enjoying my work and feeling fulfilled while I earn $450,000 a year with ease.*

Visualizations combined with affirmations pull us into a magnificent future of possibility. But they have a shadow side. And that is worry. Worrying is a powerful process of visualization that takes a negative turn. Worry is simply creating a picture in your mind of something going wrong. Visualizations are powerful. Have you ever known someone fraught with worry? Has that ever been you? You are consumed with the realness of the negative visualization that you created. Instead of allowing worry to consume you, we challenge you to use the power of creation to your advantage.

WEALTH ACCELERATOR

You have the power to pick and choose your visualizations, your worries, and your aspirations. Pick them in a way that serves you.

Not all worrying is bad. For example, worry stops you from taking unwise risks. Remember, however, you are drawn toward your visualizations. We tend to manifest our visualization as positive or negative.

> " Visualizations are extremely powerful and pull you in the direction of what you're picturing in your mind's eye."

Visualizations are extremely powerful and pull you in the direction of what you're picturing in your mind's eye. Allow visualizations to be your savior, not your jailor. Worry seems to come naturally for so many of us. But, what about equally powerful positive visualizations?

Try engaging in the opposite of worry: Create a positive visualization. Take the affirmation "I am enjoying my work and feeling fulfilled while I earn $450,000 a month with ease." After you create that affirmation, close your eyes and picture in your mind's eye where you are sitting, what it looks like, what it smells like, and what it feels like. That's all it takes—no more, no less. It is a created moment that can take you anywhere you choose to be.

CHAPTER 15

THINK BIGGER BY AIMING HIGHER

So many of our dreams at first seem impossible, then they seem improbable, and then, when we summon the will, they soon become inevitable.
—Christopher Reeve

"Knowing a lot" can get in the way of seeing new possibilities. For example, if you "know" life is hard you will not see the easy path. Learning helps you grow. A beginner's mind nurtures continuing evolution. The moment you "know" everything, you stop growing and evolving. Instead, let go of what you know to create space for something more. Here is one of the most frustrating truths: What we know now has gotten us to where we are. We have done the best we could with the information that we have. What's going to take us to the next level is not yet known to us. The skills, the experiences, and the knowing needed for our next level haven't yet been introduced to us. They're just outside of our peripheral vision. To get to that next level, we have to see what we currently can't. And that is often the great challenge in life. So how do we get to this next level?

Champions have seen that next level, which makes it easier for them to get back to it. That's why winners tend to win so much more.

And that's why people who've made a million and lost it are able to get it back again, faster than those who have never earned money at that level. They have been there, they have seen it, they did what it took to get there, they know it's possible, and all that makes it easier to accomplish. It's the certainty that they can do it.

So, if you want to get to the next level in your life, think bigger. Thinking bigger means aiming higher. Think far beyond what feels comfortable. Doing this brings to your aid forces that you don't even comprehend to help you get there.

> " By aiming higher, you will invariably discover new ways of being that let you live in a new and inspiring way."

By aiming higher, you will invariably discover new ways of being that let you live in a new and inspiring way. Did you ever hear the adage: "If you want something done, give it to a busy person?" The reason people who do a lot can do even more is because as they do more, they also grow and gain new capacities. Through perspiration, they gain inspiration. That inspiration turns around and feeds their drive for greater capacities and vision. In short: They constantly think and grow bigger.

Answering big questions will lead you to thinking bigger. In turn, the new capacities you get from thinking bigger will help you to play bigger, and you will become bigger. Think it. Then become it. What can you do to make an amazing difference in the world we share? How can you use your life to create something great that will change things and help transform the world?

WEALTH ACCELERATOR

Use the process of "Goal-Setting Through" to ensure you hit your goals. It's human nature to slow down a little bit as we approach the finish line—even Olympic sprinters tend to do this. It's why we tend to hit 85% of our goals. The solution? Goal-Setting Through: Imagine your finish line is a few steps beyond the metaphorical tape. This will carry you through the extra steps near the end. For example, if your goal is to earn $200,000 next year, we challenge you to set the goal at $240,000 and to do all you can to hit that increased number. And, if you fall a little short at the end of the year, you still will have exceeded the $200,000 mark.

CHAPTER 16

THINK 10X AND BREAK THROUGH YOUR LIMITING BELIEFS

Think BIG. There are unseen forces
ready to support your dreams.
—Cheryl Richardson

One of the biggest hurdles to building wealth is the mindset that too much would be required to have what we truly believe we deserve. We set it up in our minds that having massive wealth would require too much sacrifice. The 10X factor is a tool to break through your limiting beliefs. The 10X factor is thinking ten times higher than you currently do. And you can achieve this by simply adding a zero to your wealth goals.

We think big, but that's big relative to the people we hang out with. Do we think big relative to Warren Buffett or Sir Richard Branson or Elon Musk? I think you know the answer to that. Whenever Paul thinks someone is thinking small, he takes his own goal and adds a zero. Suddenly he understands exactly what they are feeling.

Want to know what stands in your way? Try this: Write down your annual income goal in three years and five years. Then write down your net worth goal for three years and five years from now.

Stop reading and do this quick exercise.

- Your income goal in 3 years is _____.
- Your income goal in 5 years is _____.
- Your net worth goal in 3 years is _____.
- Your net worth goal in 5 years is _____.

Can you commit to those numbers? What could stand in your way? What could stop you?

Now, go back to these four goals and add a zero. Could you commit to that? What could stand in your way? What could stop you? This is an expansive exercise designed to reveal your limiting beliefs and myths about money and wealth.

To put this exercise into focus—let's play with some numbers: Let's say your net worth is $300,000 right now—a great five-year stretch goal might be a net worth of $2 million. When you think about what might stand in your way, you might think of practical things, things that have stopped you before. But your goal with the zero added changes the conversation. Think $20 million in net worth. That may seem crazy and hard. Is it painful? What is stopping you from making $20 million your goal? By doing this simple exercise, your myths and limiting beliefs will now come clearly into focus.

What feelings does this bring up? What things do you imagine to be standing in your way? For a goal that is a reachable stretch, our limitations are less obvious. But when you add a zero it all comes into focus.

The single most-cited impediment to hitting the 10X factor is that it would require too much sacrifice. The following reaction is very common: "I am not willing to work as hard as I would have to increase my earnings goal by ten." "My family is too important to me to walk away so I can chase that goal." "It's just not that important."

" Nothing stands in your way so long as you
believe you can do it."

Consider this: Those who have one tenth of your wealth look at
you as if you have something that they lack, which is something that
stands in the way of their becoming as successful as you. When you
turn and look at someone who has 10X your wealth, know that they
are decidedly farther along in the journey. Yet nothing stands in your
way so long as you believe you can do it.

" What belief do you have right now, that if you
didn't have it, would allow you to move forward
with your amazing goals?"

Ask the following power question: "What belief do you have right
now, that if you didn't have it, would allow you to move forward with
your amazing goals?"

WEALTH ACCELERATOR

When you state your goals and affirmations, add "with ease."
This frees you from the barrier of burden and sacrifice.

CHAPTER 17

THINK DIFFERENTLY ABOUT THE RULES

It is the beginning of wisdom when you recognize that
the best you can do is choose which rules you want to
live by, and it's persistent and aggravated imbecility
to pretend you can live without any.
—Wallace Stegner

Be Aware of the Polarity

Rules guide us. They tell us who is winning, who is losing, who is right, and who is wrong. Have you ever met people who are so rules-based that they're more concerned about what's right than they are about winning the game? Welcome to our world.

Here's an example: What do guidelines like "dress your best" and "dress for success" mean? The rules tell you. In Dallas, people get dressed up. If you came to the office wearing flip-flops, your colleagues would be offended. You would be a disgrace to the profession and would be shunned. Most likely your manager would throw you out.

In Venice, California, where Paul lives, there is a different set of guidelines. Venice is the epicenter of cool. Abbott Kinney Boulevard was recently voted the coolest street in America by GQ Magazine. The vibe there is extremely casual, and the rules are just as strictly enforced by the mainstream culture, which they like to pretend is "counter-culture." Paul once watched a guy in a torn T-shirt fuss with his hair in the bathroom mirror for nearly a minute just to give it a properly messy look. This guy was a ruthless rule follower.

Paul, coming from his work in conservative Washington, DC, used to wear suits to work in Los Angeles. Whenever he did, his colleagues would tease him harshly: "Are you trying to sell caskets?" In Paul's Beverly Hills office, one of his top-selling realtors shows $20-million beachfront properties in his shorts, a T-shirt, and sunglasses while driving a 1970s Mercedes convertible. Though a bit of a rough ride, his wheels are worth close to $200,000.

In our everyday existence, we choose to either follow or defy the rules. However, you are not exercising free will in either case. The binary option to obey or resist is a polarity, and the world runs on it. Take a step back and observe this and ask: Who is right? Who is wrong? Do you want to prove it? Do you follow the rules? Do you want others to follow the rules? Or, is it the opposite? Do you break the rules? Do you want to hang out with other "rebels" like you?

Office politics are another set of rules. The guy who kisses the boss's ass gets promoted ahead of you. You can fight it, and he or she might fire you, or you can flow with it and get in line. But, are you "selling out" like the shameless sycophant? We don't believe either are shameful, because there is another choice, another perspective.

There Is Another Choice

But be aware there is another choice and that is to do something different. Simply being aware, without resistance, of the polarity as it exists can give you an edge in the game. Consider this: Be aware of what game you are playing and what the rules are. Follow the rules that help you and play along just like a rules guy. And, when the rules don't serve your higher purpose, break them.

> **"** Be aware of what game you are playing and
> what the rules are. Follow the rules that help
> you and play along just like a rules guy. And,
> when the rules don't serve your higher purpose,
> break them."

Consider Pablo Picasso's quote: "Know the rules like a pro, so you can break them like an artist." But we don't confuse his words with a lack of morality or a moral compass. To the contrary, we encourage you to take responsibility for following or not following the rules. Here's something to ponder: Are those who follow the rules in a corrupt government moral or immoral?

When we make the choice to follow if it serves us and to not follow if it doesn't, we are operating from free will. Ultimately, we are responsible. If being "right" is standing in the way of winning, let it go. Most of us want to be right. But, it's far better to win. So, if you have to let the other guy be right for you to win, give that a try—no questions asked.

WEALTH ACCELERATOR

There is a third choice, and that is choosing something different. Observe the game, master it, and figure out the rules. Follow the ones that serve your purpose, break the ones that don't, or choose a different game—perhaps your own. Know your outcome, get in touch with it. Remember it as you observe the game and the rules that go along with it. Then, make your choice.

CHAPTER 18

THINK "EASY"
INSTEAD OF "HARD"

"Things do not have meaning.
We assign meaning to everything."
—Tony Robbins

We tend to label things as hard. For example, how often do you say or think the following:

- "I had a hard day at work today."
- "My back is killing me."
- "My job is hard."

The reality is most of what we deal with is easy. We create hard by labeling things hard. For example, the other day David was served with a frivolous lawsuit. He knew that he had to spend time and money defending it, along with all the other things he was handling. He was driving to an appointment, the lawsuit on his passenger seat, a pile of white papers on black leather. He caught himself muttering under his breath about how hard his day was when he saw a guy in a wheelchair out of the corner of his eye. He turned and looked, and as he drove by their eyes met. The guy in the wheelchair was a triple amputee making his way along the pavement on a hot Texas day. It dawned on David in that instant that what he labeled hard wasn't even close to being hard.

"Hard versus easy is a choice."

Losing your limbs, on the other hand, is hard. Losing a child is hard. Work is just one task after another until we shut it down for the day. It's easy really, and it's a choice. Plain and simple: Hard versus easy is a choice. "Hard" and "easy" are simply points of view. Are you good at something that someone else finds to be hard? Is it common for you to see someone do something effortlessly that you find to be difficult? Of course it is.

Telling yourself something is hard is one of the most disabling mantras you can have. As soon as you tell yourself how hard something is, guess what? It becomes hard. Instead, try this: Over the next 48 hours, make a mental note of every time you call something hard. For extra credit, re-label it as easy. Then observe how that makes you feel.

It wasn't until we began consulting with others that we realized how rampant this flaw was. And not long after, we scratched our heads thinking, "What's wrong with them?" Then we caught ourselves discussing how "hard" it was to finish this book, and we realized, oops, we were doing the same thing! But there's a way out.

Identifying and Defeating the Enemy

How do you turn the hard things into easy things and get them done? First, if you are facing something that you believe is hard, ask yourself a few questions: Is this something I really want to do? Is this something that is key to an outcome I really want? If your answer to either of these questions is "No," then don't waste your time. Just delegate it or drop it. Wasn't that easy?

For example, paying bills on time is more of a challenge for Paul than other obligations. He hates it. It may seem small, but it isn't.

After Paul reached a point in his life when paying his bills was not a financial challenge, he still didn't always pay them on time. More than once paid his cable bill *after* they turned it off!

This quickly began to interfere with his commitment to building wealth through real estate, because investing is much more difficult and expensive with terrible credit. The "hard" conversation locked him into the "problem." As soon as he ended the conversation, new possibilities became apparent: He implemented a simple system. All bills go from his mailbox to a drawer in his kitchen. Then, his bookkeeper whom he hired to come to his house twice a month, picks up the bills and pays them. This new system costs $100 a month, and Paul has paid every bill on time for eight straight years. Problem solved and his credit is now golden.

WEALTH ACCELERATOR

What's important to you and what is hard for you? What things are hard and important? Take a stand. End the "it's hard" conversation and see what comes up!

"This Is Going to Be Easy!"

Paul remembers when a good friend was 30 minutes away from speaking at his rehearsal dinner. His friend had decided to speak from his heart and thus had not prepared anything in writing. Behind closed doors, he was freaking out and asked Paul for advice. Paul's friend had become a solid public speaker, but he had always diligently prepared. Now, 20 minutes away from his most important speech to date, he had no notes and his hands were trembling. Paul gave him the following advice: "Tell yourself and anyone who might ask: 'I'm not nervous. This is easy and fun. I am really looking forward to it.'"

During the speech, Paul's friend seemed a bit nervous, but he spoke from his heart, and everyone loved it. It was so much better than reading a canned speech. In fact, he nailed it. Afterward, he came up to Paul and said, "That was some weird mind trick you helped me play. It was so much easier when you told me to tell myself how easy it was!"

> " You don't even have to believe that easy is actually easy for you to choose it and for it to work for you."

Interestingly, you don't even have to believe that easy is actually easy for you to choose it and for it to work for you. Try it and see what happens!

CHAPTER 19

THINK ABOUT THE UPSIDE
AND THE DOWNSIDE

When the facts change, I change my mind.
What do you do, sir?
—Winston Churchill

Entrepreneurs often need to be more than a little optimistic. Feeling good about our vision helps to keep us excited and driving toward the possibility we are creating. It makes the enterprise fun: We can think how big it can become, and it's a source of energy for making things happen. But unbridled optimism can lead us astray. And when it does, we refer to it as *Hopium.*

❝ Unbridled optimism can lead us astray."

Business decisions built from a platform of delusional optimism can be a total disaster. So, we're careful to balance optimism, so it does not become Hopium! We never suggest a pessimistic approach or a focus on what doesn't work. Rather, we temper optimism by getting clarity. For every business venture or investment, we carefully think through five possible outcomes:

1. What is the worst possible outcome?
2. What is the worst likely outcome?
3. What is the best possible outcome?
4. What is the best likely outcome?
5. What is the most probable outcome?

We do this because it's a great exercise and because it helps us determine whether a deal is worth doing. If the worst-case scenario wouldn't crush us, then we move on to the next level of analysis. If there is enough upside in the probable outcome to risk the downside of a likely bad outcome, we know we can move forward and green-light the venture.

Beware of Hopium

What takes people down, and we mean *really* takes them down, is overly optimistic expectations married with aggressive expansion—in other words, pure Hopium!

Here are some examples:

- The guy who was going to open one Subway franchise instead opens five.
- The mortgage officer who was making $500,000 a year in one branch opens ten new branches.
- The day trader who makes $100,000 on a margin play, and then— high on Hopium from that big win—loses 75% of his portfolio when the market moves in another direction a week later.
- The investor who did well with one property buys 20 homes at one time, signing personal guarantees, and has no real equity in them and has zero cushion for anything other than an up market.

All of these are real-world examples that we have seen where people injected themselves with Hopium and ended up in a giant hole. They went from good businesses and great intentions to failure and significant financial losses. Why? Because they failed to measure their next step and had become addicted to Hopium.

Protect the Downside

Hope for the best, plan for the worst, and account for variable outcomes when you build your models. Let the upside carry you higher while protecting the downside. For example—

- Don't buy stocks on margin—it regularly works during bull markets and crushes people in every downturn.
- As Gary Keller taught us: Lead with revenue. Lead with revenue. Lead with revenue. The cash flow you are generating can generate more cash flow. But, don't start with huge expenses and expect earnings to catch up.
- Don't take on bigger facilities than you need. Leases are among the least flexible business costs.
- Don't over-leverage real estate to get bigger and bigger returns. Instead, make sure cash flow protects you in case of a severe market shift.
- Don't sign personal guarantees, except as a last resort.
- Don't expand too quickly.

When the real estate market crashed in 2007, David had 140,000 square feet of leased space. And, because he had personally guaranteed only 5% of that space, he, and not the landlord, was in the driver's seat. As a result, he was able to negotiate thousands of dollars of rent abatement when the businesses really needed that money.

Given the option, every tenant prefers no guarantee on leases, but here's how our approach differs from most: Right now, times are good, and landlords want or demand personal guarantees. We prefer to pay a higher rent on the lease space in exchange for no personal guarantees or to have the personal guarantee fade away (burn down) over time. Engaging in this strategy puts Hopium aside, and we pay a bit more now to greatly reduce our possible downside. If business remains good or gets better, the extra cost won't hurt us much. But if things get ugly, we're covered, and we retain the leverage to negotiate with the landlord. We find that even smart business people, in an up market, do not adequately consider downside risks and conversely, in down markets do not adequately consider the inevitable upturn coming.

WEALTH ACCELERATOR

Be upbeat and aggressive about what you're doing. Keep your feet on the ground by planning realistic outcomes. Be proactive about considering both upside and downside outcomes.

CHAPTER 20

THINK WITHOUT "HINDSIGHT BIAS"

An economist is an expert who will know
tomorrow why the things he predicted
yesterday didn't happen today.
—Laurence J. Peter

Building wealth requires predictive decisions. For example, should you invest in a particular property, stock, or business? Should you hire someone to help you? It's important to weigh a multitude of factors before deciding whether to jump in or not.

Paul is a seasoned investor with more than 25 years of experience. He bought a $2.2 million teardown for his future residence in June 2008. Looking back, the handwriting was on the wall: The affordability index was at an all-time low, indicating a major correction was likely around the corner. As it turned out, he bought almost exactly at the worst time—precisely before the Los Angeles real estate market crashed in historic fashion. A mistake like this one could teach a great lesson, or it could be paralyzing.

Awareness

It's human nature to hate to be wrong more than we love building wealth. Unfortunately, this dislike for mistakes can cause us to avoid taking the risks necessary to build wealth. Potential investors, fearful of making a mistake like Paul's home purchase, can get frozen and find themselves permanently stuck on the sidelines.

Perspective

66 After the fact, everyone is an expert."

This paralyzing fear is compounded by what we call "the flaw of hindsight" or "hindsight bias," which we define as the tendency people have to view events as more predictable than they actually are. After a specific event, people often genuinely believe that they knew the outcome before it happened. People believed they could see it coming. Endless psychological studies demonstrate this common and pervasive human error of perception. After the fact, everyone is an expert. The armchair quarterback's mantra is, "I knew it." Yet if he had known it, he could have made a fortune on that single, accurate prediction. For example, if Paul really could predict when the crash was coming, he could have bet the house in the opposite direction and made a fortune.

When markets are on the rise, everyone is a genius. All of their theories prove to be "correct," and the number of stock market day traders and real estate "flippers" balloons out of control—that is, until there is a market correction. Then, nearly all of them get crushed and disappear. Instead, we recommend that you use time-tested wealth-building fundamentals, rather than trying to time the market.

Stick to the Fundamentals

We built most of our wealth investing in real estate. We strictly follow the fundamentals outlined here and never try to time the market. Paul's large real estate buy at exactly the "worst" moment didn't hurt him in the long run because he stayed within four of his simple maxims:

1. **Buy value.** One common way to do that is to buy the worst house in the best neighborhood. Paul's purchase was the ugliest house in one of Los Angeles's best neighborhoods, and it sits at the peak of a hill giving ocean and city views. Renovating under these circumstances creates tremendous value. This inherent upside potential shielded him from the crash.

2. **Maintain a margin of safety.** Paul purchased within a margin of safety by borrowing far less money than he could have for the large renovation project.

3. **Buy only where you know the market.** Paul is from Pittsburgh and lives in Los Angeles. His portfolio is exclusively in Los Angeles and Pittsburgh. There are reasons to vary from this, but there is safety in following it.

4. **Invest only if you have cash flow to cover the mortgage.** For investment property, we only buy when cash flow either covers 100% of the costs or a short-term plan will create that cash flow. This makes our portfolios safe in a downturn. For a personal residence, we make sure we are not living in something we could not afford if the markets changed or we had a disruption in income (lost job, client, etc.).

> " By having a game plan and sticking to solid fundamentals, you will not lose in the long run."

By having a game plan and sticking to solid fundamentals, you will not lose in the long run. For example, instead of panicking and selling at a big loss, Paul continued to develop the property while the market crashed and everyone fled real estate. He kept investing in the property, because he understood and trusted his fundamentals. Now, just nine years later, the house is worth nearly $2 million more than the cost of his purchase and renovations.

WEALTH ACCELERATOR

Stick to your fundamentals and don't try to time the market. Get active, buy value with safe debt-equity ratios, and stay in the game. Over time, you will make money no matter what the market does.

CHAPTER 21

THINK PROACTIVELY, NOT REACTIVELY

Don't buy things you can't afford with money you don't have
to impress people you don't like.
—Dave Ramsey

You would think the need to keep up with the Joneses would be passé by now. One guy gets a new car, and the neighbor has to outdo him. One guy gets a bigger house, and his coworker does the same. Unfortunately, it's alive and well. Billions are spent in advertising and marketing, creating a link between buying a company's product and feeling good, being awesome, and achieving success.

This can cause us to live above our means and can put us at risk during the slightest economic downturn. Or it leaves us unable to take advantage when the market change predictably makes killer opportunities available to the few who can afford them. We have seen it happen over and over: people earning great incomes yet living above their means as if their incomes will never decrease. They have luxury suites at sports games, multiple cars, and vacation homes. And we've also seen it all come crashing down.

Letting vanity dominate your decisions can put you out of control of your financial future. We aren't saying don't buy something you want, something that brings you joy and ease. Rather, don't allow emotional reactions to rule your purchasing habits.

> 66 Don't allow emotional reactions to rule your purchasing habits."

Here's how David steers clear of the destructive path of vanity. Four times a year, he leaves the hustle and fray of his daily life to be in a place that inspires him, where he can have uninterrupted time to purposely design his life.

While he is away, he meditates on what is going great, what he would like more of, and what he would like less of. Then he pulls out his goal sheet and reviews how he is doing on what he has chosen. And he does all of this in moments of stillness, undistracted by the shiny objects that normally surround him.

During this time, David evaluates what's feeding him as well as what's depleting him. And then he chooses how he would like the next three months to go and how he would like the rest of the year to go.

He chooses his adjustments, lays down his flight plan, and then soars into his future. Some think only those who are already wealthy take the time to do this type of planning, but it's this willingness to take the time to design your life that actually leads to wealth.

If architects build homes from plans they have laid down, then you can follow suit and build your life from a plan of your choosing. Constantly check your course and correct where helpful, but do not walk through life with your head on a swivel being envious or hungering for everyone else's stuff.

> 66 If you stay centered and stay true to your evolving course, you are far more likely to achieve your goals and have what you want in your life."

Don't try to look good to the outside world at all costs while rotting away on the inside. If you stay centered and stay true to your evolving course, you are far more likely to achieve your goals and have what you want in your life. In doing so, you will free yourself from the lure of vanity.

WEALTH ACCELERATOR

Live within your means. Build your life on choices you make—not in reaction to what your neighbor chooses.

CHAPTER 22

THINK POSITIVELY, NOT NEGATIVELY

Your subconscious mind is always listening to and believing in everything you repeatedly say about yourself. So, try not to become your own enemy of progress.
—Edmond Mbiaka

Nothing will stop your progress like the brick wall of negative self-talk. So, how do we deal with this silent killer? We've outlined eight easy steps to help you get out of your own way.

> 66 Nothing will stop your progress like the brick wall of negative self-talk."

Step One: Get Clarity and Build Awareness of Your Self-Talk.

Be an observer. Identify your negative self-talk: How frequent and how severe is it? Here is a way to help measure it. Wear a rubber bracelet and give it a snap or twist a ring on your finger every time you have negative self-talk. This will bring awareness to the situation.

Step Two: Don't Universalize Negativity—Ever.

Once Paul left his antique Rolex at the Miami Airport Marriott on his way to a celebratory Caribbean destination. It wasn't the first time he'd lost an expensive watch. He's susceptible to telling himself that he "always" loses the things he loves, like his favorite watches. The voice in his head reels: *Why don't I ever lose my crappy watch? Why can't I ever catch a break?*

Here's the key. Avoid words like "always" and "never" in front of a negative statement. It locks it into your brain and becomes a part of you. Do you want to be someone who never gets a break? Of course not. And neither does Paul. As a first step, he stopped using always and never.

Step Three: Localize Your Error—Use Specificity.

On the morning that Paul lost his favorite watch, he was so concerned about catching his flight that he wasn't as vigilant as he could have been before leaving the hotel. He was able to understand the circumstances (the specifics) that led to his loss. He was frenetic that morning for a very early morning flight. Further, he implemented a plan to handle this in the future. Whenever he stays in a hotel, he places his watch in a place that will ensure it won't be left behind no matter how much he rushes in the morning.

Step Four: Recognize That "I Am" Is the Most Powerful Combination of Words in the English Language. Learn to Use These Words to Your Advantage.

Whatever follows "I am" shapes your reality. Use this to your advantage. Start by using only positive words after "I am." One of the times Paul was most angry with himself was when he was running late and got super annoyed with his dilly-dallying ten-year-old daughter. After grabbing her backpack and tossing it down the stairs, he thought to himself, "Oh my God, I am such a jerk!" Paul is not a jerk and cares deeply about his daughter. At that moment, however, he was being a jerk.

Similarly, when you say "You are . . . " to someone, whatever follows forms their self-perception. Save that construction for positive statements, and if you use a negative statement be sure to make it a temporary condition by inserting the word "being" into your speech. For example, say, "You are *being* a jerk" rather than "You *are* a jerk." Save "I am" constructions for your affirming thoughts and words.

Step Five: It's OK to Self-Correct.

> " Treat a negative thought or a setback for what it is—temporary."

Treat a negative thought or a setback for what it is—temporary. You can turn any negative into a positive in an authentic way. And, you can be tough with yourself without harming yourself. If you fell way short of your expectations, you could say: "I can do better than that!" Or, "I am powerful—there's no need to get hooked in that emotion."

Step Six: Be Authentic. Publicly Share Your Mistakes.

This is counterintuitive, because our first instinct is to hide our flaws. But if you share a mistake, it immediately loses its energy. Here's an example. Paul has a new business-consulting seminar that has received great reviews. He shares his six main points and, invariably, when he gets in front of the crowd, he can't remember all of them. So, he brings a notebook with him.

Recently, he was teaching a group of sophisticated entrepreneurs. The camera was rolling, and he looked down to find his notebook missing. Panic set in. The old Paul would have nervously begun, knowing that he was not going to be able to deliver "The Six Things You Need to Know about Business Consulting."

But instead, he said, with the camera rolling, "You know when I speak, I can never remember all six, so unless my notebook shows up, you're only going to get four or five things." Everyone in the audience laughed, and then he dived into his talk. And when his assistant rushed in with his notes, laughter ensued, and he said, "Awesome, now you'll get your money's worth. I have all six now!"

Larry King was interviewed about his lifelong on-camera success. When asked about his first big break, he told the story of how the producer grabbed him in the hallway and said there was an emergency need for him to step in for the news anchor. With no preparation or lead time, he was terrified. The first thing he said on the air was how nervous he was about the broadcast. He was surprised at how that made him feel and how the audience reacted to him. From that point on, he knew that being authentic was more important than getting it "right."

Step Seven: Understand the True Significance of Your "Failure."

For better or worse, we are far less significant than we think. You might carry around a simple blunder that caused an audience to erupt into laughter. But 99% of the audience will forget about it within an hour.

It's a fact: People just don't care about the screw-up you made nearly as much as you do.

Step Eight: Use Goal-Based Thinking.

> We don't learn when things go well—we learn when we have to revisit a decision or situation."

Ask yourself, "Do these thoughts get me closer to where I want to be? What can I learn from this that will help me in the future?" And remember: We don't learn when things go well—we learn when we have to revisit a decision or situation. What is it that you can do or be next time to get you the result you desire?

WEALTH ACCELERATOR

Even superstars don't get it all right all the time. Everyone deals with doubts. So, mess up, forgive yourself, stay positive, and move on!

CHAPTER 23

THINK THE SECOND THOUGHT

If you hear a voice within you saying, 'You are not a painter,'
then by all means paint, and that voice will be silenced.
—Vincent Van Gogh

66 It's hard to escape the trap of negative self-talk."

We all have at least a few damaging childhood memories. We felt serious pain at the time. Some of us endured physical pain, such as a beating. Others have emotional scars, like when a teacher or parent told us
that we were worthless. Some of us have experienced both or worse.
With memories like these, at times it's hard to escape the trap of negative self-talk. Even the most positive people we know fall prey to it.

As someone who is both a good public speaker and someone who
had been quite fearful of it, Paul recalls the time he had a total loss for
words when speaking to a team of frightened workers who looked to
him to lead as their Internet venture teetered on the verge of certain
collapse. Normally cool under pressure, he calmly took the helm, but
his emotions got the best of him. He remembers that so many things
swirled in his head that he just wasn't able to gather his thoughts. He
asked someone else to lead the meeting and 15 minutes later took it

over. Nonetheless, that left an impression, and it is a painful memory. And occasionally, before a speech—whether it's in front of 20 or 2,000—that feeling, that moment of perceived failure, flashes back into his mind.

Can we help ourselves from revisiting our traumas? Can we stop ourselves from having negative thoughts, reliving the darkness of the past, or rethinking about that awful thing that happened? Our trauma, whether physical, emotional, or both, is just a memory. The incident that caused it is long gone, too distant to harm us. Yet our memory brings it back, because our brains are wired for recall.

Someone trying to curb negative thinking would likely get angry. Talk about a vicious cycle—we get angry about getting angry with ourselves! Just accept that we have little power to control what we refer to as our first thought. For example, we might say to ourselves, "Damn it, I am such an idiot. I can't believe I left my watch there. I don't deserve to have nice things!" But, we can control our reaction to it. This is the second thought. And it is the second thought that matters most. We're going to show you how to win the battle with the second thought in two easy steps.

Step One: Recognize Your First Thought in a Neutral, Nonjudgmental Way.

Tell yourself, "Wow, I can understand why I might feel that way under the circumstances." Or simply recognize, or notice, that it was a negative thought or a destructive thought or urge.

Step Two: Replace Your First Thought with an Affirmation or Another Positive Thought.

Your brain cannot simultaneously hold two competing thoughts. For example, you might say about the lost watch, "Well, fortunately I have insurance," or "Thankfully, I live in a world of abundance, and yes it's annoying but this isn't a real setback." You might even say, "No one even wears a watch nowadays." Or, "It may not be pleasant, but people lose things."

If you have experienced a traumatic event, when the thought returns, you might say, "Wow, that was just awful, but it's in the past. I let that go, not as a favor to the perpetrator, but as a kindness to myself. I won't give the perpetrator power over me so many years later. And, I am stronger for having lived through it."

That's the power of the two-step process: first thought, second thought. If you choose to interpret all the experiences you have had as building you into the masterpiece you are, then each experience— whether good or bad—has contributed. In short, we cannot control our first thought, and we should not try to. So, when a negative thought arises, call it out, recognize it for what it is, and develop a replacement thought for it.

> " When a negative thought arises, call it out, recognize it for what it is, and develop a replacement thought for it."

WEALTH ACCELERATOR

You can control your second thought, and with that ability you can remove the power or harm done by any negative memory or damaging first thoughts. That way you attach only to the positive and move forward.

CHAPTER 24

THINK PAST THE CHATTER

The mind is a wonderful servant but a terrible master.
—Robin S. Sharma

Our brains are packed with 100 billion neurons, powerhouses of potential. Some 100,000 miles of capillaries and blood vessels feed the brain. Each of the 100 billion neurons has on average 7,000 connections to other neurons. The brain is an incredible organ that has enabled us to create technological breakthroughs and build civilizations. Our human mind is the most powerful of tools, and if we use it wisely, a wonderful servant!

The downside of the brain is that it never stops chattering. The brain evolved when our species had to remain constantly vigilant for protection and survival, and so its neurons fire incessantly. That's what we call "chatter." The pre-modern brain we live with was designed to keep us safe. It sends warning signals even when there is no sign of a stalking beast, creating needless worries. Our brain looks for danger. So it will tell us all sorts of things that aren't helpful to us in modern-day life. It chatters away endlessly, like a schoolboy obsessing about his first crush. Just as the mind can be a powerful servant, likewise, it can also be a terrible master. We have another choice: to stop the chatter and become its master.

> " When we catch our brain chattering away
> endlessly, that's the time to steamroll it."

In his book *As a Man Thinketh*, James Allen suggests treating your mind as a garden. He recommends that readers weed out the negative, useless thoughts, and plant empowering, fun, and productive thoughts. The idea is to stop thinking so much and steamroll the chatter. It's easier said than done and requires a lot of work. When we catch our brain chattering away endlessly, that's the time to steamroll it. Use an affirmation such as "Every day my mind is quieter, calmer, and more focused." Or a mantra like "Om." Or use music—whatever you like. We can steamroll the thoughts that do not serve us. Because if we don't proactively steamroll the chatter, then the chatter will likely steamroll us!

WEALTH ACCELERATOR

The bottom line is that we have a choice. We can allow the chatter to dominate our internal dialogue or fill that space with something that serves us. The first step is awareness. See how much chatter steamrolls your day, and then choose an alternative that would serve you better.

CHAPTER 25

THINK, "THE WORLD IS OUT TO HELP ME"

Believe that life is worth living and
your belief will help create the fact.
—William James

Good or Bad Day (Week, Month, Year, or Life)—It's Your Choice!

Do you know anyone who believes, "The world is out to get me"? Have you ever had a succession of bad things happen and even for a minute think that yourself?

Most of us have had days where it seems that everything that could go wrong did. What about the opposite: Have you ever gotten into an amazing groove when almost everything went your way—even for a little while? What if we could universalize that experience? Wouldn't it likewise be possible to conclude: "The world is out to help me"?

1. **Our Truth**: There are many thousands of forces at work every day that can affect us in what we perceive as a negative or positive way.

2. **Perspective**: If you hold either belief—"The world is out to get me," or "The world is out to help me"—it creates an expectation of the negative or the positive. Further, what you expect you will look for, focus on, and find. Every day there is more than enough negative stimuli to support a terrible day and more than enough positive stimuli to support a great day.

Getting hooked by the bad experience eliminates your ability to find, focus on, and have the great experiences that are there waiting for you. Conversely, if you allow yourself to get hooked by the good experience, it eliminates your ability to find, focus on, and have the negative.

❝ Great days, like terrible days, are a choice."

Great days, like terrible days, are a choice. Are you willing to choose to receive a good day? Days add up to weeks, weeks add up to years, and years add up to a lifetime.

WEALTH ACCELERATOR

When you hold the belief "The world is out to help me," you are more accurately creating it, which helps you. Eventually, even what you used to view as impediments will propel you to success.

The Four-Step Process to Win in Any Situation

Suppose you need to be at a critical meeting on time but you get pulled over by the police, get stuck behind an accident, or get a flat tire. It will happen. You haven't had a flat tire in years and now you get one. Is this really happening? What do you do?

We suggest following our four-step process. By doing so, you will come out a winner, regardless of the situation:

1. Focus on the big picture. Rather than focus on the obstacle (flat tire) or immediate outcome (missed meeting), focus on what you want.

2. When something or someone stands in your way, use the following powerful mantra: "This (event) has just strengthened my resolve," or "I have just strengthened my resolve."

3. Be mindful about not getting hooked, that is, emotionally tied to the "bad" event.

4. Ask, "How can this (flat tire or missed meeting) actually benefit me?"

CHAPTER 26

THINK, "HOW COULD THIS BENEFIT ME?"

You may encounter many defeats, but you must not be defeated. In fact, it may be necessary to encounter the defeats, so you can know who you are, what you can rise from, how you can still come out of it.

—Maya Angelou

You Can Reframe Even the Most Difficult Situation

As we started to explore in the last chapter, reframing gives us a choice about how to look at the things that happen in our lives. It gives us the opportunity to choose the positive in something that others would consider a negative. It's nothing short of a life-altering skill.

> We learn more from challenging and difficult situations than we do from easy ones."

We learn more from challenging and difficult situations than we do from easy ones. When we seek the lessons in what others see as "bad" or "challenging," we access an avenue that takes us to the positive.

WEALTH ACCELERATOR

One amazing way to reframe is to ask this question (over and over again): "What about this (insert awful event) is to my advantage?" "What about it serves me?" "What can I gain from this?" If you are willing to look at the most seemingly terrible circumstances and ask these questions, you have the power to reframe and reclaim power over the situation.

Here's an example of how David reframed some of his life's biggest challenges. His dad was diagnosed with lung cancer and bravely fought it for three years before he died. The last six months were very tough on the family. David chose to be his dad's number-two caregiver (behind his mom) and learned the honor that it brought to his life.

During this time, David set aside what he was doing and went to almost all his dad's doctors' appointments, including his chemotherapy treatments. Sometimes David washed his father and changed his father's diapers as he got progressively sicker. These were awful, devastating times, and they required David to take more time off from work than he had in years. Often he just hung out with his dad, arms around him, watching him slowly fade away. No one would deny this was tough.

As he reflects back (reframing), David realizes this was some of the most cherished time he had with his dad. He was grateful to have been able to give back to the man who raised him. Honoring his father in this way is one of David's proudest moments. Also, watching him fade away gave David a new appreciation for how fleeting life really is.

Before his dad became ill, David was extremely ambitious. His focus was to become a billionaire. As his dad was fading away, he decided to have a child. Life and death are so often woven together. Today he has a beautiful daughter, Isabella Grace. She is seven as of this printing, and she brings joy to David and his family. Also, when his dad got sick, David read a lot of books on health and learned about the importance of eating a healthier diet. His dad would have never taken any of David's advice. He was a meat-and-potatoes kind of guy. But David took this opportunity to evaluate his own diet and make important changes. He now eats healthier than he ever has.

As Byron Katie says, "Everything happens *for* you, not *to* you." Losing his dad was one of the hardest things David ever experienced. Now he has a beautiful daughter and better health, along with a greater appreciation for his mortality.

WEALTH ACCELERATOR

Reframing allows us to choose the positive that exists inside of every single challenge—no matter how severe. Reframing is a choice, however, and it is the choice that turns a losing hand into a winning one. Learn to reframe and you'll never lose.

Adversity Is Your Opportunity to Step Up

Have you ever heard that the Joker created Batman? Do you get it? Without the Joker, there is no Batman, because without the Joker terrorizing Gotham City, billionaire Bruce Wayne would remain in his library relaxing. There would be no need for him to suit up and fight crime. It's the Joker's reign of terror that brings Batman out of the Bat Cave.

If it is true that the Joker created Batman, wouldn't we also have a reason to thank the terrorist, the bully, or the sociopath at the office? Here's the missing piece: The Joker didn't really create Batman. Instead, he created the opportunity for Bruce to step up. But, in real life, few step up. Some could say that Hitler "made" Churchill a phenomenal wartime leader, because his reign of terror created a need, an opportunity, for a fearless leader and unparalleled orator. When not at war, Churchill was an arguably poor prime minister. But when presented with the right opportunity, he rose to the challenge.

WEALTH ACCELERATOR

When something "bad" happens, ask: "What inside of this event benefits me?" If it's awful, the answer to that question will not be obvious. Keep asking! Remember: We don't always create the "bad" event or circumstance. We do, however, create our perspective and context about it.

Heisman Trophy winner Ricky Williams told us how he wasn't the fastest, or strongest, or most talented, so we asked him what gave him an advantage in college football and then the NFL. He said he has zero fear of physical harm on the football field. He explained that as a child his mom beat him so badly, that now as a grown man there was no one who could similarly hurt him. Wow! Talk about reframing!

> " We may or may not have the power to cause our circumstances, but we do have the power to create the context and the perspective that create our reality."

Remember: We may or may not have the power to cause our circumstances, but we do have the power to create the context and the perspective that create our reality.

CHAPTER 27

THINK, "LET'S PLAY"

Yesterday ended last night. Today is a brand-new day.
—Zig Ziglar

One evening, David's then four-year-old daughter was steaming mad. They had been playing together, and he noticed that it was 30 minutes past her bedtime. David stopped the fun and told his daughter that she needed to go to bed. David knew if she stayed up much longer, she would be miserable the next day. She resisted, however, and when David insisted, she told him she would never play with him again.

The next morning, she woke up early to see David working in his office. She gave him a hug and sat on his lap. And after a few moments of yawning and stretching, she said, "Daddy, let's play a game!"

A friend of David's works in the cancer ward at a children's hospital. She said the amazing thing about kids undergoing cancer treatment was their resilience. Even though they hate the treatments and would cry while receiving them, once the treatment was over, they got right back into play mode and would say, "Let's play."

> Kids have an incredible ability to start each day fresh, renewed, and open to possibilities. That's what we call 'starting at zero.' Starting at zero every day is a choice. Children choose it, and we can, too."

Kids have an incredible ability to start each day fresh, renewed, and open to possibilities. That's what we call "starting at zero." Starting at zero every day is a choice. Children choose it, and we can, too.

If something goes wrong, even terribly wrong, like a massive business failure, a betrayal by a person or team you respect and love, or a terrible hiring choice—whatever it is—you will get an invitation to a pity party. Instead of attending, wake up, shake it off, and say to yourself, "Let's play!" When you face a major setback, you have a choice. If you view the setback as career ending, it likely will be. What if, instead, you viewed the setback as part of your amazing journey?

WEALTH ACCELERATOR

There is a genius in starting each day at zero. Approach life each day with a beginner's mind and you will learn more, see more, and enjoy more.

> Building wealth is fun if you allow it to be."

BONUS CONTENT:
THE ROAD TO WEALTH

Building wealth is fun if you allow it to be. The road to wealth is easier if you make it a game. Learn how to have fun building your wealth in the online bonus for this chapter by going to www.wealthcantwait.com/game.

PART

**CREATE THE HABITS
THAT BUILD WEALTH**

THREE

CHAPTER 28

THE SEVEN HABITS
THAT BUILD WEALTH

Success is nothing more than a few simple disciplines,
practiced every day; while failure is simply a few errors
in judgment, repeated every day. It is the accumulative
weight of our disciplines and our judgments that leads
us to either fortune or failure.

—Jim Rohn

Gary Keller starts his life-changing Quantum Leap class with this: "You don't need to be a disciplined person; you just need to master a few disciplines." That was the point where Paul said, "OK, count me in!"

Paul owns and operates a portfolio holding more than 700 apartment units. He also owns and operates ten real estate sales offices, employing more than 3,000 realtors and selling more than $7 billion of real estate a year, making him the 21st largest real estate brokerage in the United States. In the last month, he earned more in two weeks than he earned in one year as a seasoned lawyer. His net worth is comfortably in the eight figures.

Paul travels all over the world to teach and is writing this book with David with the intention of making the *New York Times* best seller list.

Today, he had his annual physical, and his doctor shared that all his bloodwork was "perfect." And, that not only had he lost 32 pounds, he had done it on a nice even progression over the last three years, demonstrating great changes in lifestyle rather than the product of a crash diet, which he had done in the past with predictable relapses.

Think about this: Just over ten years ago, when he began his law practice, Paul earned just more than $50,000, a fact one of his peer partners aptly says is "both encouraging and terrifying." Obviously, with the talent to accomplish these things, he can go much further, and he's well on his way.

Interestingly enough, Paul's also extremely undisciplined in most areas of his life. But he's mastered the disciplines, the habits that empower him to accomplish his dreams. He's adopted seven powerful habits that have transformed every area of his life, and you can do the same. Remember, it's not about discipline. It's about habits. And we'll explore each one of these habits in the next seven chapters so that you can transform your life, too.

CHAPTER 29

HABIT 1

Live Life by Design

You are where you are because of who you were. But where
you go depends entirely on who you choose to be.
—Hal Elrod

Do You Care Where You Are Going?

The reason Stephen Covey said "start with the end in mind" is because at some point if you're going to build a big life, you will almost certainly need a plan. You need a vision for your life. For some of us, this can be one of the most fun habits we have.

One of David's greatest pleasures is to go to a juice store or a coffee shop every week or so and contemplate his plan. He takes his vision and goals for his future and determines where he is and how he is doing. Then he thinks about what would improve his life and what he would like for his future.

> " To design your life with the end in mind is to create a life worth living. Being purposeful—even if it's purposefully having fun and scheduling vacations ahead of work—is the key to achieving what you want at a very high level."

Nothing is more powerful than creating a vision of the near-term, mid-term, and long-term future. To design your life with the end in mind is to create a life worth living. Being purposeful—even if it's purposefully having fun and scheduling vacations ahead of work—is the key to achieving what you want at a very high level.

The Human Life Takes the Shape of Its Context

Life takes the shape of its context. So you can either let that context be something that happens to you or something that you influence and shape. David uses his goals and vision to shape his context and his future. Obviously, he's not in control of all aspects of his future. For example, he can't control if his plane goes down, nor can he control events such as war, taxes, or natural disasters. But on a day-to-day basis he can affect what he's doing and where he's going by the choices he makes. And if he makes those choices in alignment with a path that he has chosen, a path that he has outlined, a path that he has written down, then he's much more likely on a daily, weekly, monthly, and annual basis to drive himself toward his goals. In shaping his context, he leads his life in the direction of his choosing.

This is one of the great secrets of life. Our lives are like clay, shaped by our environment. The odds are that if you are born in a particular culture, you'll like the foods of that culture, have the worldview of that culture, follow the religion of that culture, and have the economic outcome of your birth. One of the great things about the United States is that we have the opportunity to see many cultures blended into the melting pot that is our nation. Exposure to so many cultures gives us the opportunity to choose the financial and career culture we want. Bring consciousness to your life plan, vision, and destination.

One of the gifts of being an army brat, of moving more than ten times before he was 14, is that David got to see many different ways of life. He went to school in Germany, where he lived in at least five different cities. He also lived in England and went to school there before coming back to the United States when he was 14. After David graduated from college, he worked for a year, saved up all his money, and then sold everything and hitchhiked around the world for more than two years. He lived on about 20 dollars a day, or $7,000 a year. It was an awesome experience, and once again he was immersed in many different cultures and picked up many different perspectives. All of this has made it easier for him to understand the concept of context, how we are shaped by our environment, our peers, and our choices. This understanding has made it easier for him to choose to influence his own context.

Look at Yourself as Clay

> Just as Michelangelo carved sculptures out of rock, we can carve the future self we want out of the clay of our being."

We have the ability to look at our minds, bodies, and beliefs as clay. As we reshape them, we reshape our lives. Just as Michelangelo carved sculptures out of rock, we can carve the future self we want out of the clay of our being.

For decades, David always had tight calves. He would want to leap off the massage table when a masseuse got to his calves. Recently, he has been working on downward-facing dog, a basic yoga pose. He did it with real purpose and before long, he could touch the floor with his heels when inverted.

He didn't do the stretch to release tension, but he found that the tightness in his calves has diminished almost entirely. In reshaping the clay of his calves, he liberated himself from a tension that he carried for more than 20 years. Almost all aspects of our lives can be reshaped this way with enough attention, goal-setting, and accountability.

The Pivotal Moment

In Alcoholics Anonymous, there is a common saying: "I hit rock bottom." This is the place where AA knows change will take place—real, meaningful change. Someone has been drinking for decades, tried to kick the habit a dozen times, but when they hit rock bottom—that terrible place—they are finally ready for change. What is rock bottom? If you do a tiny bit of research, the horror stories flow, ranging from job loss, divorce, and domestic violence to jail sentences and near death.

WEALTH ACCELERATOR

You don't need to hit rock bottom to make a change. In fact, helping others, such as being a sponsor or a Big Brother, can add value to your life as well as that of others. There are endless volunteer opportunities out there. Pick one that resonates with you and start giving back.

Mike, the Mean Cop

Paul's dad owned a parking garage in the business center of Pittsburgh. The local policemen parked their cars there, stayed warm in the winter there, and used it as a meeting place. As a boy, Paul thought it was cool to see what police were like when they weren't giving a ticket or enforcing the law. In general, they were very nice, kind men.

That is, except for a cop named Mike. Mike was the meanest cop Paul ever met. He rarely had a nice word to say inside the garage, and outside the garage he was a terror. He gave three times more tickets than any other cop. If you were parked in a no-waiting zone, all the other cops would sternly say, "Move along." But Mike would write the ticket, slap it on the window, and then tell them to move along. Pleas from single mothers who could not afford the ticket or from senior citizens waiting in front of a pharmacy to pick up a prescription all fell on deaf ears. Mike even went as far as giving other cops tickets on their personal cars when they parked in front of the station to run in for something. His curt explanation was they weren't above the law. As you might guess, even the other cops refused to speak to him. Paul had never met a guy like Mike who was unpleasant like that all the time.

Paul noticed Mike hadn't been by the garage in a while. It turned out Mike had a heart attack. After months of cardiac rehab, he came back to work. And Paul saw a complete 180-degree change in Mike's behavior. He literally became the most pleasant man Paul had ever met. No more tickets were issued. None. Instead, Mike would run into the pharmacy for the senior citizens while they waited. "How do you do, ma'am? Can I get the door for you?" He reunited with his kids, with whom he had not spoken for a decade. He even became an active grandfather to the grandkids he had never even seen before.

Then, about two years later, the second heart attack came, and Mike died. For decades he had been the mean, brooding cop. Until he hit rock bottom. The rock bottom that changed him was the heart attack. And for about two years after, he was a changed man.

Prostate Cancer

A great guy and a close friend of Paul's was wrongly accused of sexual harassment at his law firm. The female paralegal was lazy, often complaining. She never got her work done and blamed others for her shortcomings. Paul's friend was writing her up, and she knew he was planning on firing her. She snooped through his computer and found an email where he wrote, in frustration, to a friend that she was a "bitch." Seeing an opportunity, she printed the email, took it with her, and quit on the spot. She then hired an employment lawyer and sued Paul's friend and the firm for gender-based workplace harassment.

A big firm with a solid reputation during very sensitive times, it began a full-force investigation of the lawyer and even asked him to take administrative leave without pay. Paul's friend quit, hired his own lawyer, and began a long, protracted lawsuit against his former firm. Their investigation concluded that he did not harass her. Her lawsuit against him and the firm was dismissed. And Paul's friend was hired at a better firm for more money. (So, from a legal perspective, that equals zero damages.) But, Paul's friend couldn't let it go. With more than $100,000 spent in legal fees, numerous depositions, and motions filed, the fight continued. Unfortunately, his health suffered, he wasn't sleeping, and he was crabby with his family and the folks at his new firm.

All along, his closest friends, including Paul, advised him to drop it. But, he just couldn't do it. Then after a visit to the doctor, blood tests indicated that he might have prostate cancer at the age of 45. He had a core biopsy, which was inconclusive. They decided to do minor surgery to remove part of the prostate. It turned out that the tissue removed was not cancerous. When Paul visited him in the hospital, he told Paul that he had just received the good news and that he called his lawyer and told him to drop the lawsuit.

Paul will never forget what his friend said to him: "What a difference a day can make." Just the day before he felt certain he had cancer and was embroiled in a nasty lawsuit, but the next day he was both cancer- and lawsuit-free!

We've all had epiphanies in our lives, those pivotal moments birthed in pain. While a powerful catalyst, we do not have to hit rock bottom to change. Instead, if we choose to open our eyes and learn from our experiences or the mistakes and pain of others, we can make significant changes before we hit bottom.

❝ We do not have to hit rock bottom to change."

Big Change—No Rock Bottom

Paul is fairly athletic and has played sports all his life. He's been in pretty good shape most of his life, but starting in his early thirties, he struggled to keep his weight in check.

At 6'1" with a large frame, his ideal weight is about 185—yet he hadn't weighed less than 200 pounds since high school. Instead, his weight yo-yoed back and forth. As many people do, he tried numerous diets. Every diet he tried worked while he was on it, and then be bounced back bigger than ever after going off the diet, just as the experts warn.

One day he went in for his annual physical weighing just over 220 pounds. Paul's blood pressure and cholesterol were normal. All was well except for the weight. He was pretty fit—he just had a belly. The doctor—a slim, energetic guy Paul's age—put his hand on Paul's belly and said, "Go to the cardiac catheterization lab at Cedars. The room is filled with guys ten years older than you and weighing ten pounds more. I am well aware that you love food, wine, and a having a good time, but you have to make a choice."

It definitely was not a health scare. It was barely a stern talking to. At that point, Paul made a decision: He was going to lose weight and keep it off. He is no longer on a diet. He lost the weight—a couple of pounds each week—and now weighs 185, and has for the past three years. The only thing he does is commit to weighing between 185 and 190. Sometimes he's very fit, other times not so much. But the one constant is his weight does not vary. Every day he gets on his scale, and if he's in the zone, great. He watches what he eats and he exercises, but he doesn't do anything out of his norm. And, if he wants the occasional burger, fries, and shake, he has them. But whenever the scale reads 190 or more, he has a vegan shake for breakfast, a salad for lunch, a moderate, healthy dinner with no dessert or sweets all day, and he increases his cardio nearly every day until he is down to at least 187. It only takes a couple of days, and it's hardly a punishment. He eats dessert, bread when he wants it, and pasta in moderation. But, when the scale says 190, he adjusts.

No Regrets

Want to get to the end of your journey without regret? Learn from others. Learn from their regrets. There is an amazing book titled *The Top Five Regrets of the Dying*, written by Bronnie Ware, a hospice nurse who cared for—and surveyed—people in their last few months of life. She found that dying people typically shared the same regrets. She lists the top five as follows:

1. "I wish I'd had the courage to live a life true to myself, not the life others expected of me."
2. "I wish I hadn't worked so hard."
3. "I wish I'd had the courage to express my feelings."
4. "I wish I had stayed in touch with my friends."
5. "I wish I had let myself be happier."

BONUS CONTENT: BEGIN WITH THE END IN MIND

We challenge you to follow us and create a life vision—the narrative for your magnificent life. Unleash yourself. Allow yourself to dream big. Forget constraints and disappointments. To help you visualize this, we've included our own vision statements. Just go to www.WealthCant Wait.com/XXXX to read our vision statements and to start working on yours.

CHAPTER 30

HABIT 2

Make Business Decisions
Based on Solid Fundamentals

There is not the slightest indication that nuclear energy
will ever be obtainable. It would mean that the atom
would have to be shattered at will.
—Albert Einstein

Don't Trust "the Experts"

If you want to have some fun, pick up some business magazines from right before the October 1987 crash and read what they were saying about the future of the economy. Or pick up a five-year-old issue of *Forbes* or *Money* magazine, and look at the stock picks section at the back. How many experts predicted major events or accurately picked stocks? You will find very few. How often are the experts right and how often are they wrong? About 50-50 we would wager.

Moody's, Standard and Poor's, and Fitch had rated many of the mortgage-backed securities as safe bets right up until they were nearly worthless. And what about medicine? At one time, experts recommended smoking for health reasons. Can you imagine? You can also look at the food pyramid and see how it has changed over time. Then, of course, there's agriculture. DDT was the insecticide of choice until it wasn't.

Throughout the 2016 presidential election season, experts thought that Donald Trump stood no chance. Moody's ran a model (the same model which predicted the winner of every presidential race since Ronald Reagan) that had Hillary Clinton projected to win with 332 electoral votes, leaving Trump with 206. The winner of the 2016 election? Donald Trump, with 306 electoral votes.

Our point is simple: No one cannot predict what will happen in the future. You can extrapolate from the present. You can make some general assumptions, but there are too many factors to consider. And all the experts that make "predictions" are simply making educated guesses. So, don't think that because they say mortgage rates will go up two points that they actually will. In our faith-based economy, it's pretty much all guesswork.

Our Advice

You can, however, make your business decisions based on solid fundamentals as opposed to guesses about the future. We don't base our buying decisions on future appreciation. Instead, we look for stable investments that make sense now. Our advice to you is to do the same: Invest in things that will stand up if circumstances stay the same for a long time or get worse. Have a plan that you know will create a predictable value-add. Then go for it.

> " Have a plan that you know will create a
> predictable value-add. Then go for it."

Business Moves in Cycles

❝❝ Become aware of the business cycles in your industry."

You've heard us say this before. And we're repeating it here, because it's that important. Become aware of the business cycles in your industry. While they vary enough to make it nearly impossible to determine the very top of the cycle (when you should sell) or the very bottom of the cycle (when you should buy), it can be easy to spot how hot or cold a market might be.

For example, if real estate has gone up 10% a year for five years, know that it could soon contract or fall. Alternatively, if the market's been "cold" for a while and no one is buying and prices are down 20–30%, know that things may well improve and plan your investments accordingly.

WEALTH ACCELERATOR

"I will tell you how to become rich . . . . Be fearful when others are greedy. Be greedy when others are fearful." — Warren Buffett

Be Your Own Expert—Buy Real Estate

Want to play with the big boys where the playing field is even? Stay out of the stock market, where thousands of factors weigh into a single stock's price (a single target purchase) and the broader markets are manipulated by the big players.

Instead, become an expert in a real estate. Paying a seasoned home inspector $500 will tell you more about a house (a single target purchase) than you could ever know about a stock. A very good local realtor can actually predict what the sale price of a property would be after certain improvements, or what an apartment will rent for once it is updated.

> " With very little research, you can become an expert in real estate submarkets or micro-markets."

With very little research, you can become an expert in real estate submarkets or micro-markets. (These markets are generally the size of a few neighborhoods—a smaller subsection of a city). Think about an area you know well. Then look at which parts are gentrifying. This is where there's value—regardless of what the big markets are doing.

WEALTH ACCELERATOR

Do your homework. Don't trust the so-called experts. Be your own expert and make value-based and informed real estate purchases!

CHAPTER 31

HABIT 3

Stick with What You Know and Drill Deep

What an investor needs is the ability to correctly evaluate
selected businesses . . . . You don't have to be an expert on
every company, or even many. You only have to be able to
evaluate companies within your circle of competence.
The size of that circle is not very important;
knowing its boundaries, however, is vital.
—Warren Buffett

Diversification is the closest thing to a free lunch, according to Harry Markowitz, who won the Nobel Prize for his work on the subject. For any given level of return, you can reduce the risk. And for any given level of risk, you can increase the return.

Financial Planners wisely push the idea of diversification. Diversification is rigorously described in books, charts, and articles as the long-term plan for wealth preservation. And it's true!

If you win the lottery, inherit a bunch of money, or come into a lump sum, and you haven't built a track record of success in a specific field, then by all means hire a great financial planner and diversify. This is absolutely the best tactic for you. It is the "long-term" path to wealth preservation.

> 66 If you want to build wealth, get really good at something that generates revenue and stick with it."

Just remember: Great wealth isn't built by diversifying into a million different things. This means in addition to having a diversified portfolio, if you want to build wealth, get really good at something that generates revenue and stick with it. For us, that's real estate. Real estate is the gift that keeps on giving. Real estate is where we buy, sell, and hold to build wealth. Our target rate of return is 15% a year. If you earn 15% on your nest egg, year after year, your money doubles in 4.8 years, and then that doubled nest egg doubles again in the same 4.8 years.

But that's not all. Add the notion that not only do we make good on that, we also continue to add more principal to the investment basket. Compare that to the long-term rate of a diversified portfolio of assets and you'll see why we say don't diversify.

While you are building wealth, work with a great financial planner to help you preserve it. To hear from the best financial planners, visit www.wealth.org.

WEALTH ACCELERATOR

If it's wealth you're after, build big where you can make a difference. Stick with what you know and drill deep.

CHAPTER 32

HABIT 4

Earn More by Learning More

Learning is the beginning of wealth.
—Jim Rohn

In the US economy, you get paid for your skills. Sure, some people have trust funds, some people inherit money, but for the most part, we earn by selling our skills. Keep developing your skills to keep growing your income. It also helps if you love what you do. If you bring passion to what you do, you are bound to earn more.

> ❝ If you bring passion to what you do, you are bound to earn more."

If you are resistant to learning, however, you will miss out on new possibilities. For example, David's parents often say they are "too old to change." When his mom washes out Ziploc baggies to reuse them and David tells her she can afford new ones now, she tells him that she is "too old to change." Or take the guy who hates his job but diligently goes to his cubicle every day to do what he despises under the same depressing fluorescent lights and says, "It's a paycheck." Or the woman who stays with an abusive partner and says, "I have no other choice. He provides for me, and things aren't always this bad."

Kids, on the other hand, have no problem with change and possibilities. David took his daughter Bella to an aquarium recently, and she was super excited to see all the fish. David, on the other hand, had to work on becoming excited. Kids have an innate enthusiasm for life, for anything new. This type of enthusiasm opens the door to new possibilities and expands our lives.

Learning is a choice—and so is earning. What you know now was just enough to get you to exactly where you are now. It's unlikely to get you much further. There is magic in learning. There is life in learning. We can choose to learn our entire lives, and if we do, we are choosing youth, growth, and possibility.

When we got into sales and ran our own business—where learning is most closely related to earning—miracles of learning began piling up in front of us. We noticed that what we learned and then applied to our world created results almost immediately. For instance, when we learned how to prospect for business and then actually did it, we immediately made more money. When we learned to present better, and then actually did it, we made more money. When we learned how to hire great people, and then applied ourselves, we made better hires, and our businesses got better very quickly. When we learned how to manage financials better and read financial statements, we ran a better business.

With every insight we picked up and applied to our lives, we created a better outcome. And in business as entrepreneurs, we found that knowledge can be put to work at an amazing clip. In fact, knowledge leads directly to a financial outcome. That is one of the reasons that the entrepreneurs who never quit learning build so much wealth. They keep learning so much that they outpace their peers who take less risk, and receive less reward, and are therefore not required to learn so much. If you keep learning, you will keep earning.

" If you keep learning, you will keep earning."

The same is true with wealth: Attend a seminar, analyze a deal, or read or listen to a book on wealth. It doesn't matter what you do—just budget some time and dedicate it to learning about wealth.

WEALTH ACCELERATOR

There is magic in learning. Make it a priority in your life.

CHAPTER 33

HABIT 5

Chunk Down Big Goals and Add Accountability

Sometimes our biggest life goals seem so overwhelming.
We rarely see them as a series of small, achievable tasks,
but in reality, breaking down a large goal into smaller
tasks—and accomplishing them one at a time—
is exactly how any big goal gets achieved.
—Jack Canfield

If you can chunk down big goals and be accountable for them, your life will change. Paul attended and graduated with honors from three schools with three degrees. He has a degree in Economics from the University of Pittsburgh, a master's in Industrial Relations from Oxford University, and a juris doctor from Cornell Law School. His experience at Oxford was effortless for him. His experience getting his other degrees were "beyond awful."

> " If you can chunk down big goals and be accountable for them, your life will change."

The difference in his experiences was not discipline or brain-power. He had the same amount of discipline and ability throughout his academic career. The difference was what we call "chunked-down accountability."

WEALTH ACCELERATOR

Create chunked-down accountability. Break big projects and big goals into bite-sized pieces with the help and support of strong accountability. To make it stick, throw in a healthy dose of major celebration for hitting each step.

Here is how this played out in Paul's schooling. He was always an extreme example of a leave-it-till-the-last-minute-to-finish, study-the-night-before-the-exam kind of person. He struggled in college and law school. Law school was the worst, because the way it was structured enabled him to procrastinate the most. At Cornell, like most law schools, nothing counts except for the final exam. There are no midterms. There are no graded assignments. All the classwork, all the notes, assignments, etc., counted for nothing. Everyone's grades for the majority of the courses were based 100% on the final exam.

Because no work is truly required before the exam, the impetus for Paul to do anything other than wait until exam time was nil. And he came through as expected, having done nothing the entire semester as he entered finals. The awful all-nighters he experienced as an undergraduate turned into a solid two-week exam period cram session with almost no sleep. He would study 20 out of 24 hours, cramming for the exams. It was painful and awful. It's true that he created the problem—law school was just the perfect storm for procrastinators like Paul.

But his master's degree from Oxford University, which was after his undergrad difficulty and before his law school nightmare, was an absolute breeze. There were no all-nighters, just mild review. And he aced the final exam—coming in second place in his class. What was different about his experience? And what did it teach him?

Oddly similar to law school—and perhaps more extreme—the entire degree, pass or fail, was based on two solid days of closed-book exams taken in a special location, while wearing a special exam-taking outfit. A nightmare for the procrastinators, right? Not this time.

As at other schools, Paul skipped most of his classes. But once a week, every single week, all the students had a semi-private meeting with a single designated professor called their "tutor." This tutor was assigned to two students, and the three of them met each week. In the meeting, their tutor gave them their assignment for the following week, which was a long essay question on a topic they were covering that week in classes. During these sessions they would read aloud the previous week's essay for comment and critique provided by the tutor and the other student.

Paul met with his tutor every Thursday. Every single week, he waited until the last possible moment before he would pick up the essay question and the reference manuals to find the answers. He would read the question, panic, skim the books from the reading list, and begin writing. There would be a very late night on Tuesday, followed by more studying and another all-nighter on Wednesday. He would draft the essay and proof it through the night. Thursday, he would proof his essay, go to the meeting with his tutor, read his essay, listen to the other student read theirs, and get critiqued and graded. But the grades didn't count for anything. Then, he would give the professor and the other student a copy of his essay.

At the end of the year, rather than prepare an entire year's worth of study before the exam (which would have proven to be all but impossible) all he did was read his essays, his tutor partner's essays, and the professor's comments. He poured through them and reduced them to note cards. By the time his exams came around, he had spent all his time creating the cards but almost no time to review them. In the end, he aced the exams. It was not until much later in life that Paul realized that the Oxford method forced him to compartmentalize his course-work. He broke it down into several mini-exams, which made the end-of-the-year review a breeze. He had never been so well prepared. He didn't even need to study.

People look at wealth building as a single event, but this is a mistake. We suggest you look at wealth building as a process, not a single event. Part of that process is chunking down your big goals into small, bite-sized ones and then adding accountability.

Accountability Brings an Objective Perspective

David used to gamble, but he rarely won, so he stopped gambling. He was accountable for his results. If you want to achieve your goals, you must be accountable for your results. Have someone you can talk to. Someone who will hold you accountable to your investment decisions and wealth-building goals, preferably a friend or colleague you can rely on to be real with you and help you stay the course.

> ❝ If you want achieve your goals, you must be accountable for your results."

If you ask people in Vegas how they are doing, most of them seem to say, "Oh, I am up just a little bit." Obviously this isn't true: Most people don't win in Vegas. So why is this the most common response? We believe there are two reasons.

The first is that no one wants to be seen as losers, so they would rather lie than tell the truth (even to themselves). The second reason is that people remember their wins more than their losses. They may forget they took $300 out of the ATM and figure that because they won the last two hands and have $200 bucks in their pocket, they are up a bit. A peer partner will help you look at this dispassionately. They will have the benefit of perspective. That objective perspective can help you make millions. So, if you are struggling with your goals, get a partner to help hold you accountable.

BONUS CONTENT: HOW TO CHUNK DOWN BIG GOALS

To dive deeper into how Paul chunked down his big goals at Oxford and how he now applies this effective strategy to all his business endeavors, check out this exclusive audio, which you can access at www.wealthcantwait.com/chunk.

CHAPTER 34

HABIT 6

Spend Less Than You Earn and Invest Your Leftover Cash

Financial peace isn't the acquisition of stuff. It's learning to
live on less than you make, so you can give money back and
have money to invest. You can't win until you do this.
—Dave Ramsey

Sounds simple, doesn't it? Yet so many people increase their spending as much or more as they increase their income. The culture we live in encourages spending: We are made to believe that we need a new car, a new TV, a new set of clothes, a new everything. We are not proposing you live life like a pauper. That's no fun. But if you don't save some cash, you will not have anything left over to invest.

The wealthy live off cash flow from their investments (or invested cash). Learn from them. Put your money to work. Think of your extra dollars as employees, and if you put them to work for you, they will one day pay you all you need to live and more.

66 Put your money to work."

For example, say you earn $6,000 per month and only spend $5,000 of that money. By spending less than you earn in one month, you just built $1,000 of wealth by practicing one of the simple habits of wealth building. Now, put that money to work for you. Over time you will build a small army of dollars working for you!

Keep some emergency cash for unexpected expenses and invest the rest. Where you invest your money is entirely up to you. But, it's extremely important to know your industry. That's where research comes into play. If you're just getting started, seek out the help of a qualified financial coach if you are unsure of where to invest. One thing is certain: Money left on the sidelines does nothing other than wither with inflation, becoming worthless over time.

Don't make the mistake of thinking you have to be wealthy to invest. Imagine being a lifelong janitor and gas station attendant. Working 40, 50, or even 60 hours a week to make ends meet. For every 50 dollars you earn, you invest 40. This is exactly what Ronald Read of Vermont did. When Mr. Read passed away at the age of 92, he left behind an $8 million fortune by simply spending less than he earned and investing the rest.

If you don't want to invest most of your earnings like Mr. Read, you can start small. Are you a smoker, for example? *The Millionaire Next Door* shows how a small amount of money over the course of 46 years can grow into a sizeable sum when invested. Say, for example, you are a heavy smoker and smoke at least three packs of cigarettes a day during the week. Three packs a day over 46 years invested wisely in a portfolio would exceed $2 million! If you're not a smoker, maybe there's another habit you can give up or modify, so you can invest the rest.

The worst thing you can do is nothing, because even in losing you are gaining knowledge that can help you perform better next time. But if you never start, you never gain.

WEALTH ACCELERATOR

For the next 90 days, practice living like the wealthy. Create a budget and develop an investment strategy. You can start small. Save a percentage of your money during this time and research a few different ways you can invest it. After the 90 days, look at your savings and weigh your options. Do you have enough to invest in some stocks? To increase your contributions to your 401(k)? Or are you inspired to keep saving for an even bigger investment, such as starting your own franchise or investing in some rental property?

CHAPTER 35

HABIT 7

Let Go of the Small Stuff

The biggest obstacle to wealth is fear.
People are afraid to think big, but if you think small,
you'll only achieve small things.
—T. Harv Eker

For Scale in Business

You can't grow big if you work small and manage small. You have to understand small and have systems for small, but you can't manage small if you want to grow big. When David first got a checking account and a credit card in high school, he blew them both. He violated Habit 6 by using his credit card to live beyond his means. But he learned from that. Especially after his folks refused to bail him out, and he had to sacrifice the little luxuries he had come to enjoy at an early age. His dad taught him to balance his checkbook and not live off credit. So, he applied that. And guess what? It worked. He didn't overdraw his account again, and he kept his credit card use to a minimum. He balanced his own checkbook for years. It served him all the way up until he had his fifth rental property.

> ❝ You can't manage small if you want to grow big."

Then he realized he was never going to invest again if he had to manage his own rentals. At some point, you just cannot do more. Just like in high school, he was blowing it again. This time he was overextending himself by taking calls about things that annoyed him at all hours of the night and day. He soon realized that he couldn't grow big by managing small. Instead, he would have to delegate small to grow big. So, he hired a property manager. And instead of selling all his rentals, he built his rental portfolio up significantly to where today it grosses close to $900,000 a year and nets approximately $500,000 a year.

For Sanity in Life

Once David was driving down the street and a guy cut him off. Another time a key employee, whom he had treated amazingly well, left him for a "better" opportunity. Both of these events upset him. Have similar things ever happened to you?

Have you ever noticed how even the smallest things in life can "hook" you? These events are like hooks that get under our skin, pull us off balance and off our game. The thoughts from these events can be like spinning wheels in our heads, taking us out of the present and into a wasteland of angst. When this happens, we have another choice—to unhook.

To do this, stand up and imagine the side of your hand is a Ginsu knife with a blade that is forever sharp. Then allow your mind to run free and allow any preoccupations that you may have to bubble to the surface. For example, think about what your agenda is for the day. Think about your family, your workout, the guy that cut you off, and all the calls you need to make to build your business. Then take your hands and karate chop the air around your entire body. Do not miss any part, whirl your hands around like you are a ninja. Cut all those made-up energetic pulls from your force field and unhook from all those seemingly important but mostly imaginary issues that prevent you from being fully present and purposeful.

Try not to judge this activity. Sure, it might look silly or seem stupid, but it is less silly and stupid than getting hooked and pulled off your game. So, give it a fair shot. Something else to consider: All those events that threw you off your game are based on stories (your perspective) that you made up. What if you allowed for an alternate perspective? For example—

- Maybe the guy who cut you off was late for work and about to get fired if he was late one more time.
- Maybe missing that promotion was really a blessing, because that job really wasn't a good fit for you, or that department was about to be downsized.
- And maybe losing money on one deal was actually "tuition" for an education that could save you tons of money on a later deal.

Once you're unhooked, you can be objective and open when you evaluate your life's path. When you've cleared away all that psychic debris, you can be fully present to play with your child or have dinner with a loved one or to simply have some downtime to regroup. We are not suggesting that your worries or problems will magically go away. We are simply saying that the habit of cutting the cords you accumulate each day will help you reshift your focus, reclaim your center, and get back to what really matters: your life, the way you want it.

WEALTH ACCELERATOR

Living unhooked is a great way to stay in the present. You can do that by using the Present Time Consciousness (PTC) mantra. The PTC mantra will help you maintain a more equanimous state, free of worry or concern for the future.

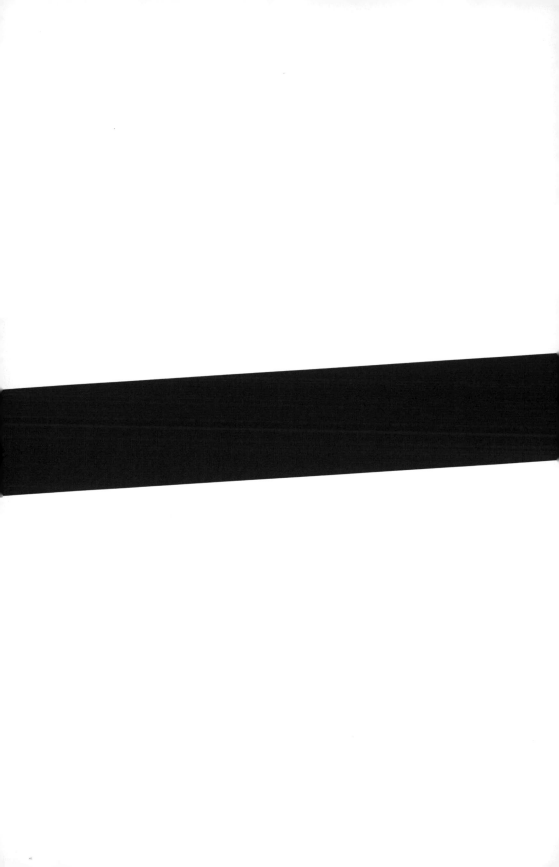

PART

DEVELOP A BUSINESS
THAT BUILDS WEALTH

FOUR

CHAPTER 36

PILLAR 1

*Client Acquisition Is King—
It's the Most Important Skill*

To me, job titles don't matter. Everyone is in sales.
It's the only way we stay in business.
—Harvey Mackay

In Part 4 of this book, we offer you the Seven Pillars of Business to understand your business and evaluate new opportunities. If you master the Seven Pillars, you will become an A-level businessperson.

One Skill Counts When It Comes to Successful Businesses

The first pillar of business is this: She who controls the client, controls the business. Plain and simple. When we say it like that, it seems obvious. But we challenge you to ask any professional what it takes to be super successful in their field.

❝ She who controls the client, controls the business."

Guess what the lawyer says? Be a great student of your particular area of the law. Be a great negotiator and advocate. Be great in front of a jury. Know exactly how to put a complex deal together.

Guess what the realtor says? Know your neighborhood better than anyone else. Be an expert with the sales contract. Listen to client needs. Know how to anticipate issues that come up in escrow. Be a great negotiator.

How about the surgeon? She would say to know how to save lives, right?

Be aware that people often confuse being great at what they do with what it takes to be super successful. They list a bunch of skills that make for an excellent practitioner, but that misses the point. If you want a profitable business, focus on acquiring and retaining clients. Client acquisition is the first rule for having a successful business.

Do you think that being an amazing lawyer, a great surgeon, or a skilled realtor gets you all the clients you want? It doesn't. That's what people say when they refuse to acknowledge the truth. The truth is that the business (or activity) of acquiring clients is not the same as doing a good or even great job on your clients' work. Without clients, everybody starves.

If the client doesn't know you exist, it doesn't matter if you're the best surgeon of all time, an unbeatable lawyer, or an amazing realtor. The primary business of any profitable entity on the planet is finding (and keeping) clients.

Rainmakers Rule

If you graduate first in your law school class at Harvard, join the most prestigious firm in New York, and then grind out 16-hour days of hard work and on-the-job training for eight to ten years, they may make you a partner in the firm. That partnership—the "golden ring" at law firms—entitles you to a middle office with a window and a very nice compensation package. But it also commits you to a lifetime of work-weeks of 60+ hours and intense pressure.

We liken it to a huge pie-eating contest where the winning contestant obtains the right to eat more pie. And why does this law firm get the right to ask for 60+ hours a week for life from you? Because they have the clients. They have already built a pipeline for client acquisition by making client acquisition a priority.

Paul was working in one of these law firms. He saw it play out with the smartest and hardest-working lawyers, only a few of whom made partner. Then one day, after several months at the firm, he noticed he had never seen the occupant of the huge, well-decorated corner office. An assistant sat outside that door, sometimes making calls, sometimes writing letters, but he never saw the partner who "occupied" that office.

When he asked, he was told it belonged to someone who had a similar office in several of the firm's other locations. She brought massive corporate clients to the firm—Fortune 500 companies who spend millions of dollars per year on legal services. In law firm parlance, she was a rainmaker. She didn't practice law; she brought the clients and made sure they were happy with the firm's work, not her work.

If the ace lawyer from Harvard, the partner with the middle office, decided to leave the firm, he would have to shop around for another position, showcase his talents, and hope that he would fit in somewhere else. His partners would hate to see such a nice, smart worker-bee leave. But, they could replace him. However, if the rainmaker decided to switch firms, the entire firm would be in a panic. Rainmakers are very hard to replace. The rainmaker, unlike the worker-bee, would make appointments at which the firm, not the lawyer, would put on a dog-and-pony show to demonstrate its worthiness to handle the work of rainmaker's client. Then, once the rainmaker was satisfied that the firm would take great care of her client, the law firm would have to figure out how many millions to pay her and what perks they would give her to "close" her to come to the firm.

Of course it helps to be a great lawyer in addition to being skilled at acquiring clients—but we want you to recognize the undeniable truth: Client acquisition is king in business. If you don't get this, don't start a business.

❝ Client acquisition is king in business."

We've both built very successful real estate franchises. We own some of the largest franchises in the country for residential sales. We have built our businesses by mastering the art of getting great agents to join our firms. We have taken it further by mastering hiring leaders who are great at client acquisition. Many people have come and gone in our world. Some may be brighter, better communicators, more hardworking perhaps; but if they don't master client acquisition, they don't last in our business.

WEALTH ACCELERATOR

When you bring in the business, you rule the business. You are the boss. You call the shots. Plain and simple.

CHAPTER 37

PILLAR 2

Look for Barriers to Entry

In investing, what is comfortable is rarely profitable.
—Robert Arnott

In business, it's important to understand the fundamental concept of barriers to entry. Paul understood how to apply this law in every area except his own; it took him years to figure out how it applied to real estate. This was primarily because he saw cash and credit as barriers to entry. But they're not. The truth is this: Without a barrier to entry, money will flow to an opportunity until it drives the rate of return down to a normal—that is, low—rate of return.

We are always looking for amazing opportunities, which means they generally must have a significant barrier to entry. Cash and credit are not significant enough to act as a strong barrier that increases rates of return to a point that is of interest to us. Instead, we look for those investments that have more significant barriers.

Following are some examples of common barriers to entry:

- **Training and/or expertise.** For example, it takes 16 years of training, and significant brainpower, to become a cardiac surgeon.

- **Government regulation.** Paul bought a mental healthcare facility, and the red tape is enormous. This deterrent will keep most people out and drive up returns. Other forms of government regulation include licensing and patents, because you have to pay someone to allow you to use their process.
- **Economies of scale.** This applies differently in different business sectors. For example, in automobile manufacturing it costs millions of dollars to make one car, but the costs per unit decrease as you produce more.

A barrier to entry is quite simply what stops outsiders from entering your market. If you have no market protection, your business likely isn't viable, or at least won't produce great returns over time.

> " A barrier to entry is quite simply what stops outsiders from entering your market."

Real-World Examples

There are low barriers to entry for realtors. That's why there are so many of them. The possibility of high commissions coupled with low barriers brings in the masses. Thus, you could easily guess that the field would be overcrowded, and it is. So, should you avoid being a realtor? At first look, yes, but let's dig deeper.

You don't want to be a realtor just to be a realtor. Likely you want to be a very successful realtor. There are more than a dozen $1-million-commission-earners working in Paul's offices. Their willingness, day after day, week after week, year after year, to spend two or more hours a day actively, purposely, and intelligently generating new business sets them apart from their competition. Lead generation, doing the "push-ups" of client acquisition, is *the* barrier to entry to being a very successful realtor. That's the truth, plain and simple.

Let's apply the barrier to entry principle to an unrelated business.

Paul had a top realtor come to him for advice. Tired of the grind (client acquisition) that took him to $600,000 a year in commissions, he was considering opening a Menchie's franchise (a spinoff of a now ten-year-old tart yogurt craze). His reasoning was, "You should see the lines down the street at Pinkberry, and now Menchie's does the same thing, only better. And they have lines of customers, too."

The first thing Paul told him was, "Please hear me. I know *nothing* about the food service business and nothing about the yogurt business. But if you're still interested in my advice, it's this: I think it's a terrible idea, because it takes capital, time, and effort (these are small barriers when profits run high), and there are zero significant barriers to entry."

Sure, you have to sign a lease, but there is nothing to the product other than frozen sugar and milk. So long as there are supernormal profits in any of these brands, outsiders will view the low barrier, and they will enter the market again and again until profits drop and become far less interesting. And many will go out of business in the process. Since then, Yogurtland, FroYo, and numerous other brands have joined the fray. And guess what? There are no more lines at Pinkberry or Menchie's because many of the yogurt shops are going out of business.

So, are barriers to entry good or bad? There are no great businesses without them. If you want a real advantage and a great business, you have to seek out a significant barrier to entry. Let's go back to real estate and look for barriers that are significant enough to create a huge profit.

Right now in Beverly Hills, if you own a building that is in good condition and is predictably fully rented, you can command a sales price so high it drives the return to the new buyer down to between 2% and 3% (decidedly not extraordinary). So, in a good market, money and credit are not significant enough to generate extraordinary profit. Following are two case studies in which our real estate investments encountered and overcame significant barriers to entry to create extraordinary profits.

Case Study 1—Due Diligence Before Bidding— Lower Barrier to Entry

Paul's real estate group was a bidder in an auction liquidating the assets of a very large trust. This auction required buyers to purchase "as is." In most transactions, you have a short period to inspect the property after you get an accepted sales contract (called the due diligence period), and you can back out of the deal if you find something substantial, such as a weak foundation, a mold infestation, or a severely damaged roof. But in this auction, you could only spend time and money to examine the property before the bidding. Thus, you could waste a lot of time and money and end up getting outbid. This is a small barrier that lowers prices a bit.

The trust had several Class-A properties, each of which had hundreds of units and were highly sought after. They had great locations, were well rented, and in fairly decent condition. Cash and credit proved to be an insignificant significant barrier. The bids on the properties submitted by Paul's group, while slightly higher than normal, weren't even close to the winning bid amounts due to the low barrier to entry and increase in competing bids.

Case Study 2—Unusual Obstacles/Ugly Duckling— Higher Barrier to Entry

One of the trust sale properties Paul's group was looking at was very suspect. It was in an excellent location, had 100 apartment units, one house, and 100,000 square feet of retail commercial. All of it was slightly run-down. You would expect money to flow toward this deal and drive down the return. Without any serious issues or barriers, this property would have easily sold for $4,000,000 at that time.

There were, however, two serious issues with this property. First, there was a dry-cleaning plant that worried potential buyers who were concerned about complex environmental issues. Second, the entire property was heated by an 80-year-old boiler plant located beneath a public street. The boiler plant structure was compromised, and the city had cited the property as a possible public hazard, putting the street above at risk of collapse. Without solving these issues, banks would not lend. So, this deal appeared to be a cash-only deal, which was another huge barrier.

Now, do you run from these barriers or run to them? Paul's group knew zero about environmental risk and zero about civil engineering. Yet they can assure you that the following process was not rocket science. Rather than immediately pass, or decide to bid very low to account for a wide array of potentially costly outcomes, and the need for a massive amount of cash to close, they looked further.

A small amount of research led them to discover that the government had a program, which, among other things, licensed specialty environmental consultants to examine possible toxic risks. If these specialized consultants gave you a clean bill of health or a list of issues to remediate and you fixed them, they have insurance and a government program that will guarantee you against future liability.

Paul's group contacted one of these consultants who looked at the property and quoted $20,000 for the certified investigation and report. This wasn't a small amount of money for them. Then they contacted reputable engineering firms large enough to evaluate and fix the boiler plant and assure the integrity of the street. They needed an estimate that the engineering firm could guarantee—that is, the amount they quoted would need to be enough to fix the problems sufficiently to satisfy the city and make the property one that the bank would lend for. But this brought yet another big hurdle: The firm had to do lots of work—core drilling, for example—just to provide such an estimate. The firm wanted $25,000 just to do the comprehensive report.

So they faced another fork in the road: Do they invest $45,000 into testing on a property they don't have under contract—with the risk that testing might yield massively bad news? This was a tough one for Paul's group. They were helped along when a friendly, aggressive competitor—who had won some of the other bids—revealed that it would be bidding at 40 cents on the dollar for the property. So, based on the huge potential upside, Paul's group went for it.

Here are the results:

- First, the $20,000 environmental testing yielded no toxic issues—not only did they have a clean bill of health, they also had a guarantee against later issues.
- Second, after $25,000 worth of testing, the engineering company gave Paul's group a bid to repair and make the boiler plant safe, reporting that it would cost $125,000 to shut down the plant and make the street safe. Because updating the heating was a huge value-add, they knew that shutting down the plant was the way to go.

Armed with this information, Paul's group bid and won the property for $2.4 million. They had spent about $60,000 on due diligence and needed $125,000 to shut down the boiler plant plus $200,000 to put in new heating throughout the project, which added additional value. Thus, by capitalizing on the barrier to entry, they bought a $4.5 million property for around $2.8 million. Totally worth it.

CHAPTER 38

PILLAR 3

Magnify Your Effectiveness and Power through Leverage

Leverage is the reason some people
become rich and others do not become rich.
—Robert Kiyosaki

A business is scalable. For us, the best business is one that can run without you. To do that you must have amazing leverage.

66 The best business is one that can run without you."

There are at least three types of leverage:

1. Systems leverage
2. People leverage
3. Financial leverage

Each of these types of leverage magnifies your effectiveness and power to make an impact. In building a business, you should consider using all three types of leverage.

Systems Leverage: Defining and Following Standards

David grew up a rebel. His dad was a Green Beret colonel, so they had a lot of discipline at home. This caused him to want to test boundaries at school. He was not afraid of teachers, and often, to his later chagrin, not very respectful. He hated the rules and went out of his way to break them.

Today, David and his team find many rules liberating. They find choosing the correct "rules" and mutually agreeing to follow them accelerates their success. Here's how: In a sense, what they know as "rules" are really just "standards." In one of David's businesses that bought, sold, rehabbed, and/or turned homes into rentals, he processed more than 600 homes in five years. In one year alone, he bought more than 300 homes. When you go from doing 1 or 2 rentals a year, which is all he did for the previous 15 years, to doing more than 300 homes in a single year, your world radically expands and demands on your time explode.

How do they keep up with the expansion? How do they handle the increase from 1 to 2 homes to buying 300 homes? In a word: rules (or standards). David's team created a well-defined standard for each scenario, and those were the standards they applied. They had—

- Standards for the homes they would flip
- Standards to determine which of the homes they would keep as rentals
- Standards regarding home acquisition
- A standard and process for how they would bid on the homes

Becoming rule-bound is a choice. In the same way we evaluate the property inventory we keep, our workouts, and even our relationships, we have a set of rules for how we treat each other in our "tribe." David went from a guy who hated rules to choosing to be rule-bound, because he saw the value in operating based on parameters. That's because the parameters enable the expansion.

WEALTH ACCELERATOR

If you are a natural rebel, don't overlook the value of being rule-bound.

People Leverage
Your Team Determines Your Wealth

Military training dictates that an optimal number of direct reports is five. The quality of your business life is a direct result of the talent level of those five direct reports. Even the CEO of a massive corporation can effectively lead with only five direct reports.

Many years ago, David took a class from Gary Keller about how to identify and hire great people to work in his organization. It was early in his career. He was 29 years old. Jack Welch describes the importance of hiring top people this way: "If you pick the right people and give them the opportunity to spread their wings and put compensation as a carrier behind it, you almost don't have to manage them."

> If you pick the right people and give them the opportunity to spread their wings and put compensation as a carrier behind it, you almost don't have to manage them."

Gary had David draw a circle and then drop five lines from that circle to five bubbles. "OK," he said, "Now who do you have working for you? These are your wealth determiners." At that time, David was a realtor working in Austin, Texas. He had made one hire, an administrative assistant whom he had met because she drove a golf cart where he played. She seemed nice enough, but it didn't work out.

She was worse that terrible because she was fairly effective when she was on task, but she was only on task 50% of the time. Her competence while she was on task lulled him into believing she might work out. If she were not competent at all, he would have come to the obvious decision earlier: He needed to fire her. He didn't want to treat anybody poorly or let anybody go, so they coexisted for nearly 18 months.

Needless to say, by the time David took this class, "the student was ready." He drew one circle under his name, and it was her. The realization hit him hard—there was no way he could carry out his vision of an awesome business with her running his admin. He needed to fill those five boxes with some serious talent. With that realization, he went straight back to the office and wrote out a plan on how to get out of business with her.

Then he went about hiring talent. He failed many times but made it his mission to become great at identifying and hiring talent. Over time, he's made some great hires and some mediocre ones. He became so committed to this concept that he made his number one business goal in life to have five direct reports who made over $1 million a year. He knew if he could achieve this, he would be very successful. And having that goal attracts major talent.

So, what was the outcome of David's plan? Today, he has three guys who run businesses for him who make more than $1 million a year, so he's 60% there. And his organization has close to 15,000 people in it. Just imagine where he will be when he gets those fourth and fifth spots filled!

The Process of Creating a Great Team

When creating a great team, use Paul's notion of being rules bound when hiring. Develop standards in advance and stick to them. You might miss some great hires, because they fail on certain fronts, but it is better to pass on a few good ones than to hire a single bad one.

Hiring is an art, not a science. People look at Paul's team and think, "Wow, you are surrounded by superstars. No wonder you create great results." And then time and time again, people try to duplicate this and fail.

❝❝ Hiring is an art, not a science."

Here is what his administrative team looks like: He has a senior staffer who has been with his company for more than ten years. She is beyond world class, and he pays her well. Paul knows what she wants her future to look like, and he's helping her get there. He's also had an executive assistant for more than five years. They have never had someone like her on their team before in this position. She's a rock star. That's the truth—and that's what it looks like from the outside.

Here's what people don't see: the years—not months—where he had one failed executive assistant after another. The average lasted six months. Paul remembers how nervous his current executive assistant was at the six-month mark. He had the reputation of "being such a great boss," but then coming in and firing his executive assistant a couple of times a year. Five years later, that is completely forgotten.

Paul uses the same hiring process for his leadership team:

- Find the best.
- Find out what motivates them.
- Hire them.
- Create an environment that supports the new hire.
- If they are working out (perhaps not perfect, but on the road to meeting standards), they keep working together.
- If they're not working out in 90 days, he fires them and starts over.

Paul hates this process. He hires people he likes and whom he believes will add value. But, he is committed to hiring "world class." In Paul's business, the mission-critical position is called team leader. Team leaders generate the business for his offices. Paul has five world-class team leaders. The longest member has been with him for more than ten years, and the newest has been with him for just over a year. Very few people in the entire company (aside from David) have folks like these, let alone five of them.

What people don't realize is that Paul does make hiring mistakes. People just don't notice or remember them. If Paul's hire is not world class, he lets him go quickly. When Paul makes a great hire, he does everything he needs to do to keep them. He discovers their dreams and aspirations. He figures out how to be a vehicle to get them to where they want to go. He wants each of them to earn more than $1 million a year. Each member of Paul's administrative team will eventually earn more than $100,000 a year while building wealth inside Paul's company.

WEALTH ACCELERATOR

Get the right people, in the right positions, under the right conditions.

 Get the right people, in the right positions, under the right conditions."

How to Determine the Right Position

First, we determine where we need help. Let's say, for example, you're running a pretty good business, but it requires you to be a jack-of-all-trades. And you're earning $80,000 after you pay all your bills.

In this scenario, you might need to net $75,000 to pay all your personal and living expenses. So, you have only $5,000 to invest above your bills and lifestyle. It might seem counterintuitive, but your first hire would likely be an administrative hire. And, a great administrative person might cost $40,000 a year. So, you've just effectively lowered your net to $35,000. Now you're making less than your new administrator and putting yourself $40,000 a year underwater at your current lifestyle.

This is the "reason" people use to not make their first hire. It's also why they don't transform their job into a business. Here's what we have to say to this: First, you don't truly invest $40,000 on your new hire. You only invest $10,000 for the first three months of the administrator's salary. Second, the administrator should free you up to go much deeper into your core competence, the areas that make you money. If after three months you aren't on a path to making an additional sum that is at least twice your administrator's salary, you either have the wrong person or the wrong business model.

> ❝ The first business of business is client acquisition."

Remember Pillar 1: The first business of business is client acquisition. This is your top priority. If you are running to Staples, making copies, and doing other administrative tasks, you're not using your time effectively if your goal is to take your business to the next level. It all boils down to this one question: If you had more free time, would you be able to use it to acquire new clients? If so, hire an administrative assistant and put them through the test.

How to Find the Right Person

Once you determine the right position, you must find the right person. We study this extensively and teach the hiring process. Here are some of the most important things we look for when hiring people to join our team:

- **Look for a track record of success.** If someone sounds great but has bumped from job to job and never really made it anywhere, run from them. Don't hire someone you need to fix.

- **Get a resume.** Make sure to dig into it and do research to verify it. Are there gaps in the resume? Before the actual hire, spend the money to run a credit check, a background check, and look at their online presence. What do they post on social media? Are they a good representative for your company? You might say, "Well they're a sales person, why should I run their credit?" Paul doesn't refuse to hire someone because they have bad credit, but he runs it anyway, because it's an important topic for exploration.

- **Check references.** Very few people actually do this. When Paul checks references, he reads his questions from a sheet to make sure he doesn't miss anything. Then he always asks, "Who else knows Sally?" Then he takes those self-generated references and calls them. Everyone should give you a list of references who will give them glowing reviews. But, once you go two or three deep—asking references for more people who know the candidate, and then asking those people—you move far enough away from the source to get real, credible reviews.

People say, "Well, nowadays, does anyone really tell you the truth and risk a lawsuit just to give bad reviews?" Just do it. We promise, you will be surprised. Paul has skipped this step before. He loved the person. They were smart, awesome, and killing it at a major competitor of his. But he didn't call their references, and he got screwed big time—a $1.2 million theft that was avoidable. And, that monetary loss was just the tip of the iceberg. When you consider the disruption of business, time required to fix the mess, and sheer stress of it all, the loss was more than double the money that was taken. Do yourself a favor. Take a class on hiring. Reach out to us at www.wealthcantwait.com, if you want to learn more on where to take it.

WEALTH ACCELERATORS

1. **Hire problem solvers.** Problem spotters are a dime a dozen. You want someone with critical thinking and problem-solving skills on your team. Not someone who only knows how to point out a problem. The problem solvers will help take your business to the next level with their valuable contributions, freeing you up to focus more on what you do best.

2. **Hire intelligence.** How do you determine if they are smart? Ask tough questions. We learned to ask a few questions that the candidate would not be able to answer. You aren't looking for the "correct" answer. That's not the point. Instead, you want to find out how they think. This will also let you see what they do when they are under pressure and are faced with a question they simply cannot answer. For example, do they fake it? Do they try to work through it and then admit they don't know? Or do they come up with a creative solution that you haven't even considered?

3. **Follow Rick Pitino's mantra.** Hire "PhDs"—those who are Poor, Hungry, and Driven. They don't have to be financially poor. Just be certain they have fire in their bellies. Pitino passes on the lackadaisical super talents and recruits very good talent with fire in their bellies.

4. **Use a behavioral profile.** We recommend the DiSC profile. This online personal assessment tool will increase your ability to hire and keep great talent. It will also help you discover if the candidate will likely succeed in the position.

Financial Leverage
Use the Right Kind and the Right Amount of Leverage

Real estate investment has the advantage that banks commonly loan money toward its purchase. This gives you the opportunity to add financial leverage to a real estate deal, lever up your rate of return, and control more assets with less of your own capital invested. Because real estate is an asset lenders readily understand, you can borrow at relatively very low rates.

If your return on capital invested increases based on the leverage you get from a bank, then you have something called positive leverage, meaning the more you borrow, the better your return. The question becomes how much leverage is the right amount? If the return keeps getting higher, shouldn't you borrow 100% of the cost of the real estate asset?

Our answer to this question is almost always "No." We balance the increase in yield based on borrowing versus the amount of risk of borrowing more money. As long as your property cash flow (income less all expenses) pays all of your bills, including the mortgage (with some cushion), then you are using a safe amount of debt. The goal is to be close to bulletproof in each asset while still getting the advantage of leveraging with debt.

We know many smart people who got crushed in a downturn. That breakdown comes when they are over-leveraged in a real estate investment, and the market corrects downward, creating negative cash flow and negative equity in an asset. The pain of that financial pressure causes other good assets to get sucked into the bad assets vortex. Suddenly their real estate empire caves in under the pressure, and the investor goes bankrupt or takes severe net-worth damage, because their real estate portfolio had a built-in requirement for positive or neutral growth to sustain itself.

If you have equity equal to 20–30% in every real estate asset you invest in, then you will have a cushion against a shift in the market. If you see the shift occurring, you can still get out of the asset without writing a check, and/or you'll have better cash flow, so if your rents go down you can still cover the debt.

Normally, financial institutions secure debt in two ways: They secure it with the underlying asset, the property. Thus, if the borrower fails, they can take over the property, sell it at auction, and keep the proceeds up to the amount of the loan. They also require a personal guarantee, meaning you personally guarantee the loan for any shortfall when the foreclosure/auction sale doesn't satisfy the entire debt. In this instance, the lender can come after as many of your assets as necessary to cover that debt. It is this personal guarantee that takes down investors in a recession. One terrible development deal crashes and the lender goes after all their assets. It can, and has been, devastating.

More sophisticated investors can get something called "non-recourse" debt. Non-recourse means banks cannot go after your other assets, and require only the underlying property to secure the loan. This is generally available only to very large investors who put enough money down so that the lender is not at risk of loss if the economy tanks.

Leases and Personal Guarantees

Leasing a space is also a form of financial leverage. If you lease and build out space for your business, you are using the building owner's money to leverage out your operational hub. Keep in mind that a lease, just like a loan on business equipment, is another example of leverage that can help you expand when you don't have cash available to do it, but also can take you down during a recession.

Most leases come prewritten with personal guarantees in them. Here is our advice: Do not sign them. Negotiate them away if you can. This is much easier to do in a downturn than in a booming market. It is also much easier to do for a business that has a track record of success than it is for a new or struggling business. Either way, during lease negotiations you should try to get rid of any personal guarantees.

Think of it this way: Your business is like a giant ship in the ocean. If it stays afloat, you will make money. But if it sinks, then any personal guarantee is like a rope tied around your waist connected to the ship. It will take you down with it if you let it. So, cut those ropes.

In the case where a building will not release you from a personal guarantee, negotiate a declining guarantee where each year you're in the building, the personal guarantee declines, or negotiate a buyout that lowers each year that you operate. David tries to go 100%, 80%, 60%, then 0%. If you operate so that you can manage your downside, the upside will take care of itself.

> " If you operate so that you can manage your downside, the upside will take care of itself."

Why do these things matter? In the last downturn, David had 140,000 feet under lease, and only 5% of this space had a personal guarantee on it. When a couple of the businesses he owned started losing money and he had to renegotiate rents with a tough landlord, he told the landlord: "Do me a favor and lock me out." You don't have the luxury of taking that position if you have signed personal guarantees. In that case, David ended up getting a 75% reduction in rent for a couple of years from a landlord who would have given him zero if David were on the hook for the lease. David has a friend who signed an $18,000-a-month lease during the boom with a personal guarantee with no cap or burn-off. The business failed. Fortunately, they were able to reduce their losses by subletting the space at $12,000 a month for the next four years.

CHAPTER 39

PILLAR 4

*Modeling—Identify a Person or
Company That Is Doing What You
Are Doing at a Much Higher Level*

If I am walking with two other men, each of them will serve
as my teacher. I will pick out the good points of the
one and imitate them, and the bad points of the other
and correct them in myself.
—Confucius

Identify Best Practices

Want to quickly take your business to the next level? Identify the person or company that is doing exactly what you're doing, but at a much higher level. See what great things they are doing that you are not.

> ❝ Want to quickly take your business to the next level? Identify the person or company that is doing exactly what you're doing, but at a much higher level."

Recently, Paul was looking for a new client interface for his real estate syndication business. He searched the Internet for a dozen high-end investment firms, from small to large, and looked at their websites. He was interested in finding out if they had a client portal. And if so, he wanted to know what it did and if it was intuitive.

Does this seem like stealing? He's not ripping off their design. He is merely observing what several top firms do and seeing which of those ideas work for him. Plus, he's adding his unique expertise to make his the best out there.

WEALTH ACCELERATOR

Use the sweat of someone else's brow to advance your business, otherwise known as "not reinventing the wheel."

Find Someone Who Is Killing It

Paul was recently consulting with an ear, nose, and throat doctor. The doctor was looking for best practices—in other words, how to make more money, more efficiently, without seeing more patients—which for her generally meant working longer hours. Paul told her to find and ENT who was "killing it," who has more years in their practice, and who would sit down and share what they knew. The doctor was perplexed, "Why would they want to help me? This is a competitive business."

The doctor's concerns may be warranted. However, she may also find someone who would gladly help her; she has to ask to figure that out. Second, she can always find someone outside of her competitive area, if she does not find anyone nearby who is willing to share their success stories. Fortunately, at the next national ENT conference, the doctor found a fantastic businessman/doctor and asked him out to dinner. She said it was one of the most valuable business meetings she had ever had.

In many fields, especially sales-related professions such as real estate, best-practice seminars are given all the time. If you aren't in a field where people regularly share best business practices (for example, medical doctors have many seminars on the latest techniques but relatively few on building their businesses), then go to the seminars anyway, find someone who is doing great in your field, and ask them to dinner.

WEALTH ACCELERATOR

Don't presume that someone won't want to share. Most people love to share their successes. Go to seminars where speakers are talking about things that can improve your business. Seek out these speakers and ask them to spend an hour with you over coffee or lunch.

When you meet that amazing person or speaker and you want to take them to lunch, say the normal complimentary things, share 15 seconds or less about yourself, and then say: "How can I earn the right to take you to lunch?" Or if applicable try, "I heard you are an amazing wine collector. What is your favorite bottle?" Then send it to the speaker and ask them to lunch. You'd be surprised how often this works. When you find a possible source of valuable information, such as a speaker or someone who has knowledge specific to your industry, ask for their help. Make an effort to build a relationship with them. It will reap great rewards.

" When you find a possible source of valuable information, such as a speaker or someone who has knowledge specific to your industry, ask for their help. Make an effort to build a relationship with them. It will reap great rewards."

CHAPTER 40

PILLAR 5

Invest in Your Area of Core Competence

Risk comes from not knowing what you're doing.
—Warren Buffett

It seems pretty basic—hard work in the area of your expertise pays the most dividends. Take Steve Jobs's advice: Don't chase too many rabbits. Use focus and simplicity to gain success.

> " Don't chase too many rabbits. Use focus and simplicity to gain success."

Nike's CEO Mark Parker once asked Jobs for advice while they were both onstage at a business conference. Jobs said he had one piece of advice for Parker: "Nike makes some of the best products in the world—products that you lust after. But you also make a lot of crap. Just get rid of the crappy stuff and focus on the good stuff." Recounting that uncomfortable moment, Parker noted, "He was absolutely right, we had to edit."

As described in the April 2012 issue of the *Harvard Business Review*, Apple was failing before Steve Jobs returned in 1997. When he resumed his position as CEO, he evaluated every single product line and reduced his findings to a simple, yet effective message that he shared with each of the department heads at their first meeting, "The products suck and you have too many of them." He then proceeded to reveal how he would fix their problem by getting back to basics: Consumer and Pro, Desktop and Portable. Chase too many rabbits, you starve; chase one, you eat. After his return to Apple in 1998, Jobs reduced Apple's product line from 350 to 10! It was their first major step back to success.

Sometimes it seems that getting out of your core competence comes from boredom—just as you finally get great at something, you want to move on. In *Outliers*, Malcolm Gladwell found 10,000 hours on the job to be the single greatest factor correlating to massive success. Most of us get bored and move on long before we hit those 10,000 hours.

Our core competence is our 20%. It is where we are we generating most of our results. It is the space where we have the potential to create something truly great. It's where "awesome" resides. It's fascinating, because that core competence can deceive and elude us. One factor that contributes to this is that experts in a particular field not only know the field the best, they are also intimately familiar with its challenges. These experts might advise us to go in a different direction (one they don't know as well) simply because they're so aware of the challenges in their industry that they forget the opportunities they have gained from their focus.

Who, other than a realtor, understands better how tough it is to deal with clients, close a deal, get a loan, or get a price reduction? But from the outside, we look like overpaid salespeople. What about doctors? Paul has several in his family. And guess what? They tell their kids not to be doctors. They're all too familiar with the insurance hassles. "We don't make nearly what we used to make. One little thing goes wrong, and you get sued. And now Obamacare!" Their list of reasons not to enter the profession is long and persuasive.

> " If you want to go far, invest in your area of core competence."

If you want to go far, invest in your area of core competence. That's what we do most often. Does this mean you should never invest outside of what you know? Here's our advice: Study and apply the Seven Pillars of Business. At the very least make sure you're investing with someone who is in their own core competence and has a track record of success in that area. And then make sure they have skin in the game.

One of the toughest investors Paul knows just invested with him. The investor knows Paul has a great track record. And he knew the area (but not the pricing) as well as or better than Paul, so he knew the project was in a great neighborhood. But, he didn't have access to the same deal flow and didn't want to be the lead investor when he knew Paul could run the deal at a high level. Rather than do a deep analysis of the deal (which Paul expected him to do), he simply said, "I will do this deal without all the due diligence if you put in one-third of the capital. If you do that, I know based on your track record you believe in the deal, and I am in."

WEALTH ACCELERATOR

Savvy investors bet on the person they are investing in as much as they bet on the deal. So, when you are looking for your next great investment, be sure to look in your own backyard before you fly off to invest in a copper mine in Peru, no matter how good it sounds!

CHAPTER 41

PILLAR 6

Use the 80/20 Rule to
Drill Down to the Vital Few

The few things that work fantastically well should be
identified, cultivated, nurtured, and multiplied.
—Richard Koch

Eighty percent of our results come from 20% of our efforts. This
prolific rule has been applied in numerous contexts for more than
100 years. In 1906, economist, sociologist, and engineer Vilfredo
Pareto discovered that 80% of the land was owned by 20% of the
people in his home country of Italy. He came up with the mathemat-
ical formula to represent this unequal distribution of wealth while
he was gardening. There he noticed that 80% of the peas came from
20% of the pods. The 80/20 rule was born from that level of diverse
observation, and it persists. Everywhere you look you will find appli-
cations of the 80/20 rule.

66 80% of our results come from 20% of our
efforts."

Later, Dr. Joseph Juran, a quality management guru, applied Pareto's law in business, coining the phrase "the vital few and the trivial many." The 20% are the "vital," and the 80% are the "many." He found that 20% of the errors caused 80% of the problems, and 20% of the employees caused 80% of the errors. If you drill down to the vital few—both good and bad—and take action with that focus, change will come rapidly.

Applying the Pillars

The most important rule of business is Pillar 1, "The Real Business of Business is Client Acquisition." This is the first place to apply the 80/20 rule. Keller Williams Realty International teaches our realtor clients to touch their database 33 times a year. Some of it is automated—monthly newsletters and email blasts—but other parts of the 33-touch program are highly personalized: birthday cards, calls, and in-person meetings. When realtors analyze their business, they will find that 80% of their business comes from 20% of their clients, and 80% of their clients come from the top 20% of their referral sources. We all have limited time and resources to spend cultivating business, so use it where it counts most.

So, if a realtor were to have a database of 1,000 potential clients and referral sources, they should not be treated the same. They should prioritize their database and identify the top 20% and touch them more frequently and more personally. Likewise, they can save money by taking the bottom 20% and either cutting them out entirely or keeping contact with them only through automated systems.

You can apply this to any business. For instance, Paul was helping his friend who owns a digital media agency. Paul gave him an assignment to look through his client database and determine where all his clients came from. Then Paul asked him to start with the top 20% of his clients—those who regularly use his company's services, buy more products, pay their bills on time, are nicer to work with, and refer more friends. Then, he told him to take his current database and determine where his top-quality clients came from. His friend was surprised by some of the results and not by others. In any case, they were able to create a plan of action for him, so that he could continue to attract his target clients.

Paul took the agency's top two and bottom two sources for getting new business. The bottom two were tossed out completely. For example, the agency quit doing certain types of online marketing. This method was expensive and yielded few quality clients. Then Paul identified the top two methods of client acquisition—referrals and seminars that the CEO taught. The agency then created a client appreciation program for those folks who referred great clients to him and was more purposeful about doing his seminars, increasing them from four per year to one a month.

Within six months, the agency's business grew by 15%, and that 15% was made up primarily of high-quality patients. Just like the agency, 20% of your customers or employees will cause 80% of your problems. Just as we use the 80/20 rule in a positive way, it also works in the opposite way. For example, these bottom 20% of clients will cause a disproportionate amount of trouble, headaches, and unpaid invoices. Consider dropping these clients to spare yourself the emotional, physical, and financial drain.

Not-to-Do List

WEALTH ACCELERATOR

Good to Great author and management guru Jim Collins suggests making a "Not-to-Do" list. This practice is a perfect use of Pareto's law. While you are prioritizing what "To Do," you can also take the time to look at which of your activities are the least productive and eliminate them.

A good friend of Paul's who has grown as a businessman to the point where his time is quite valuable was still spending several hours a month sitting with his wife paying the family bills and entering them in Quick-Books. This is an activity they both found stressful, bickered about, and did not enjoy. Realizing that paying the bills was an item on his "Not-to-Do" list, he decided to hire Paul's bookkeeper to come to his house and organize his monthly "shoebox" full of receipts, pay his bills, and reconcile his household bank account. By identifying what he doesn't want to do and finding a viable solution to this problem, Paul's friend has just freed himself up to spend the time he used to devote to book-keeping to other activities that he finds more enjoyable.

Make your own "To-Do" and "Not-to-Do" lists. Maybe you'll dis-cover it's time for you to hire your own assistant, even if it's a part-time or virtual assistant. Paul just sat on a plane with a young lawyer who had left a big firm to go out on his own. The lawyer retained some import-ant clients but was doing all the work himself with the help of only one secretary. In addition to doing legal work, which he could bill for, he was also doing non-billable paralegal work. During their conversation, it became apparent that it was time for the lawyer to hire a paralegal to free himself up do to more billable work. This simple realization, made by creating an informal "Not-to-Do" list, would increase his profits while affording him more time for his family.

WEALTH ACCELERATOR

Get outside help. Hire a consultant, a coach, or just ask a smart friend to chat with you about best practices in your business. In part, you are doing things the way you are doing them because you think it is the best way. That's OK. It makes sense. Now, get outside eyes to help you find ways to better focus your efforts on what matters most.

CHAPTER 42

PILLAR 7

Invest in Coaches, Mentors, and Masterminds

Each person holds so much power within themselves that
needs to be let out. Sometimes they just need a little nudge,
a little direction, a little support, a little coaching,
and the greatest things can happen.
—Pete Carroll

You Need Coaches
Yes, YOU!

Most people don't have coaches. Most people also don't have what they want in their lives and are not on the path to achieving it. Just over ten years ago Paul had barely heard of someone hiring a business coach or a life coach. And when he finally did hear about it, he thought it was ridiculous.

If you had two soccer teams with identical talent, and one had a coach and the other didn't, how would you expect the results to come out? We think you know the answer to that—so if you think your kid's second grade, part-time, after-school soccer efforts are worthy of a coach, why would you think that your life's results are any less worthy?

We think the answer to that is that we somehow see needing a coach to guide us through our lives, our business, or our work as juvenile or a sign of weakness. Instead, we should just man (or woman) up and do what we need to do to take care our business.

All Top Performers Have Coaches

So why does the greatest golfer in the world employ up to five people on his coaching staff at a time? Novak Djokovic, the number-one tennis player in the world, just added a third coach to his team. We can guess what you are thinking: For the number-one golfer or tennis player it makes sense, and for your second-grade soccer team it makes sense too. It just doesn't make sense for *you*.

WEALTH ACCELERATOR

The best accountability partner is a skilled coach who not only holds you accountable but also brings perspective and resources to the table.

Simply hiring someone to hold you accountable will change your results dramatically. The coach is invested, because her livelihood depends on the success of her clients. So, select a coach who knows your area well, and your results will skyrocket.

> " Simply hiring someone to hold you accountable will change your results dramatically."

Andy Murray, the second-rated tennis player in the world, finally won his first Grand Slam after hiring Ivan Lendl as his coach. Lendl, once a young, undisciplined, and spotty player with incredible skills but mixed results, hired a coach named Wojtek Fibak. Later in Lendl's career after he'd become world class, no one remembered the hit-and-miss version of his earlier days. Fibak is single-handedly credited for taking Lendl from the promise of youth to a star who would prefer to crush the life out of his opponents rather than just beat them. During his career, Lendl was not liked. He was feared. And he also won eight Grand Slams.

Andy Murray—an incredible player who always came up short—had gone to the finals all too many times without winning a Grand Slam. Then he hired Lendl as his coach, and within two years he won both the US Open and Wimbledon, becoming the first Briton in 77 years to win Wimbledon. Murray always possessed the skill. But he gives much of the credit for his added toughness to the single act of hiring Lendl as his coach.

If coaching is closely linked to the outcomes of the top sports players in the world as well as those of second-grade soccer players, your career and life are also important enough to warrant an excellent coach. Adding a professional business coach was a watershed event for Paul as he climbed from having no money to entering in the top 1% of income generated from passive sources alone. Coaching provided him, among other things, with accountability and a third-party perspective.

Take the First Step

> " Take the first step and find a good coach today."

Take the first step and find a good coach today. By asking around and doing a little research, you will find the right person to motivate you and help you succeed. If the coach doesn't prove helpful, you can easily make a change. In our opinion, nothing brings more purposefulness to your life and business than hiring—and paying for—someone whose sole responsibility (at least during that call or meeting or training session) is to hold you accountable and facilitate your success. Your life is worth that level of purposefulness.

You Need Mentors
Mentored by a Billionaire

One of David's greatest blessings as an entrepreneur has been the coaching and modeling he has received throughout his life. One role model was a man destined to be a billionaire: Gary Keller.

Gary is a natural teacher. In David's business career, nothing has influenced him more than the insights he received from Gary. Gary's commitment to learning, setting goals, and taking action have had a huge effect on David's business success. Even more important, David had the opportunity to be around a guy with a mindset of wealth. The influence that experience has had on his own mindset is huge.

When he was 15 years old, David's mom joined Keller Williams when it was a start-up real estate company. She was the seventh agent to join the business, which was founded by Gary Keller at the young age of 26. Gary and David's mom built a strong and enduring relationship around the growth of the company, which eventually went on to be the number-one real estate company in the world.

After he graduated from college and hitchhiked around the world for two years, David began working for his mom in real estate as her assistant while he looked for "a real job." It's funny how so many people end up in real estate by default rather than design. Joining the Keller Williams team allowed David to be taught and mentored by Gary.

First Lesson: Lead with Revenue

"Lead with revenue," Gary told him. "Never let expenses get ahead of your revenues." What Gary was saying was you cannot count on running any business for long if your expenses exceed your revenue, so at the end of the day, you should always lead with revenue. If you spend less than you earn, you can keep your business going indefinitely.

> " If you spend less than you earn, you can keep your business going indefinitely."

Second Lesson: Set a Vision for Your Life

In 1994, Gary was teaching a class on goal-setting. The class was called "Quantum Leap," and there were about 20 students in the class with David. Gary passed out a handout with the following question: "If you were to meet me here in two years, what has to happen for you to look back on your life and say, 'The last two years have been amazing because I . . . '?"

There were 24 lines to fill in with things to accomplish over the next 24 months.

It was a difficult exercise for David. He had taken some classes here and there, but overall he wasn't an avid goal-setter back then. So, he ground his way through the exercise, eventually coming up with 20 goals that he thought were pretty cool. Some of them he had thought of previously, but most of them he just made up during the exercise.

After the class, he took the piece of paper home and shoved it in his desk drawer, placing it mindlessly in his "for later" file. Time went by and pretty soon he had forgotten about the exercise. He was getting on with production, lead-generation, sales, and enjoying his life. About a year later he was clearing out his desk drawer, which was now full of paper in the "for later" file, when he came upon that goal sheet. And he was surprised to find that he had accomplished about 10 of the 20 items on that list without even thinking about them again. That was an epiphany for him.

"If I got 10 out of 20 done without even looking at the list," he said to himself, "how many could I get done if I actually paid attention to it?" And seeing as how he had thought up some of those goals in that class and now those "creations of the mind" had been achieved, he wondered what would happen if he devoted himself more purposely to creating a future of his choosing.

From that moment forward David became an avid goal-setter. And he's never looked back. He's become a man who achieves a lot of his intentions every year, a guy who hits the mark he sets far more often than not, and a man who has an amazingly rich life in the areas of importance to him: health, wealth, and adventure. One of the key reasons for this abundance is that he sets 30–40 large goals every year and completes 75–80% of them.

Third Lesson: If You Do Not Have an Agenda for Your Life, the First Person You Meet Each Day Will Give You Theirs

> **If you do not have an agenda for your life, the first person you meet each day will give you theirs."**

Gary Keller says this all the time. It ties into goal-setting. If you're not purposeful in your goal-setting, you won't have your daily agenda. Instead, you'll be aimless, and if someone with a purpose meets you, they'll give you their purpose for the day instead. Being authentically purposeful with your goals and your life makes your life more fulfilling, because you will attract people, work, and activities that are in alignment with your purpose.

You Need Masterminds

In Napoleon Hill's classic work, *Think and Grow Rich*, he says this about the power of masterminding: "When there is more than one gathered together, the power of the group is multiplied *exponentially*."

Imagine if you were constantly hanging out with Warren Buffett, Bill Gates, and Jack Welch; what are the odds you would be poor? Or if you were hanging out with Olympic athletes as friends, what are the odds you would be in pretty decent shape? The questions answer themselves.

" We are who we hang out with."

We are who we hang out with. Jim Rohn, author and motivational speaker, tells us that we are the average of the five people we spend the most time with; so if you want an incredible life, doesn't it make sense that you should build your own tribe of winners, a tribe of people who want the same things you do? This is the essence of a mastermind.

The guys David hangs out with are financially free, so it would be odd if he didn't achieve financial freedom, too. The guys in his mastermind work out consistently. If he didn't work out all the time, he would not fit in with his community. That's what's so great about a mastermind: You get to pick your tribe, and the better the tribe, the better your results.

Masterminding Produces Results

David can attest to the power of masterminding. His two peer partners are very physically active. He was not. He worked out, but it was not a deeply ingrained way of life for him. Going to the gym was a struggle. Tim, however, lived to ski, mountain bike, and climb in the backcountry. Pat loved to do marathons and run with the charity called "Back on Your Feet." They were both more physically active than David was. Over the last 15 years they have built all their mastermind retreats around physical activity. They almost always climb a mountain, hike, or ride a bike someplace. David had to step it up if he was going to keep up with his peer partners. Today he works out 250 times a year and is in the best shape of his life. If he didn't hang out with Pat and Tim, he knows he wouldn't be in such great shape.

How many world-class organizations operate without a board of directors? Is there a single one? So how do you operate a big life without a board of directors? That's what your mastermind is, your chosen group where "normal" is building passive income and wealth.

Here's another example. When David was younger, his mastermind focused on hours worked. They worked their butts off. That's how they competed. How shortsighted was that? But guess what? They worked like crazy, because that was their tribe. Today they still work hard, but now they focus on passive income and dollar-productive activity. They went from being grinders to working smart. And they did it by constantly asking the question, "Is this activity going to get me where I want to go?"

> " They went from being grinders to working smart. And they did it by constantly asking the question, 'Is this activity going to get me where I want to go?'"

The other gift he gets from his mastermind is that they are all committed to contribution, to giving back, and both of his closest peer partners do a lot for others. That is also part of his tribe and community. Because of his peers finding a way to give back, he has easier pathways to give back as well.

So, create a vision for your life. Build a community around you that stands for your success. Implement a schedule that keeps the focus on your goals and form a community where winning in your field is the norm. Then doing amazing things will be your new normal!

You Need People Who Believe in You
Surround Yourself with People Who Believe in You

Your relationships should be with friends who uplift and encourage you. You need to have people who offer solutions, not complaints. You need to have people around you who do what they say and say what they mean.

Paul remembers telling his shrink about ten years ago, "Well, if I just make this small change and that small change, then my business would grow, and I could do X, then Y, and then Z, and it would affect my world in the following ways." She said, "Yes, but you can't do those things." Paul was horrified. He asked her, "How do you know?" She responded, "Well, it's obvious that if you could do those things, you would do those things. But, you can't." It wasn't long after that he fired her. Perhaps he should send her a thank-you note, because it spurred him on to surround himself with people who *did* believe in him!

WEALTH ACCELERATOR

Get rid of the people in your life who are sure you cannot accomplish your goals. Get into relationship with people who are certain you can accomplish your goals. It makes no difference if you have to hire your own "fans."

Beware of Energy Vampires

Do you have people in your life who wear you out? Stress you out? Make you feel guilty? Leave you feeling angry or "less than"? You may be dealing with an energy vampire. This is a well-documented phenomenon, and there are several types. These three are the most common:

1. **The Victim** blames anything that they perceive as not going according to their plan as the result of something or someone else. It can be extreme—actually nothing is ever their fault, ever. They also are eager to tell you the *real* cause of their maladies and provide loads of evidence to prove it.

2. **The Drama King or Queen** makes everything hyperbolic. Their emotions run hot with lots of ups and downs and almost never a period of calm. "You can't believe what happened on the way to work this morning!" Paul knew one Drama Queen who loved to throw gasoline on someone else's fire. She would observe drama and inflame it.

3. **The Guilt-Thrower** though closely related to The Victim, this one is a little different. They're absolute experts at making everything your fault. They're virtuosos at making you feel bad about something. Family members are often experts at doing this.

Avoid Energy Vampires

So now that you can spot an energy vampire, the next step is to follow our simple rule: Walk away.

Knowing that Paul is in a people business, a well-meaning friend recommended a book on how to deal with difficult people. Instead of reading the book, Paul told his friend, "No, thanks. I avoid difficult people."

When Paul talked to a wise friend about his difficulty in just walking away, Paul said, "Well, I feel badly for him. I don't want to hurt him further, and I do care about him." His friend said, "OK, but you do realize that he doesn't care about you, don't you?" Paul replied, "How do you know that?" His friend's answer was profound, "If the energy vampire cared, he would be sensing your discomfort rather than just dumping his on you. He would ask how you were doing, and he would care about your answer."

Energy vampires don't care about you. They care about managing their own discomfort, and they have found that zapping others makes them feel better—albeit very temporarily—because it does absolutely nothing to solve their issues.

Energy vampires are experts at sucking you in by asking for your advice. When you give your thoughtful advice, they respond, "Yes, but . . . " and tell you why that won't work for them. Nothing you say will help them.

Tricks for Dealing with Energy Vampires

One person Paul knows never, ever has a positive thing to say. As soon as he approaches, Paul says to him: "Hey, John, great to see you! Tell me something good!" The look on John's face is priceless. He has no idea what to say. Then, when Paul refuses to do the usual negative engagement and asks again, "What's good in your life, brother?" John finds him annoying and walks off.

When dealing with energy vampires, don't defend. No matter how crazy another person's attack, if you defend it, you are giving them the energy they desire. When you defend your position, you're playing their game by their rules. You may think you can prove them wrong—but it's not the "rightness" or the "wrongness" they truly desire, it's the engagement or the fight they truly seek. They would love it if you were to agree with them. However, disagreeing is a close second best, because they want the attention, the engagement, and the fight. Even if you can't escape, you don't have to engage in their negativity.

Paul remembers one family member saying to him, "You know, you'll never, ever change." This angered Paul. It took a little while for him to realize the obvious: Inside that statement is the assertion that Paul is not OK the way he is. So instead of getting hooked, he just agreed with the energy vampire, which withheld the engagement they sought. Because he's OK with who he is, Paul just said, "You're right. I'll probably never change." This left Paul empowered and the energy vampire surprised and confused.

The next time you're confronted by an energy vampire, instead of getting hooked, slow down, take a deep breath, and smile whether you want to or not. Then, you can deflect without engagement, saying something like, "I'm sorry you feel that way. I want you to know that I listened and heard you. You won't convince me, and I won't convince you. So, we're going to have to agree to disagree. I won't discuss this further." Then hold your ground. If they persist, say, "Sorry, this conversation is over. Now, tell me something good!" Dollars to donuts, they'll flee like a vampire seeing a cross.

LIFE TIP

When dealing with energy vampires, remember that you're always in control. Don't give them power over you. Instead, cast them out of your life by disengaging and walking away.

BONUS CONTENT: HOW TO SET UP YOUR OWN MASTERMIND

If you're not already part of a mastermind, or know of one you'd like to join, then just form your own. We assembled some quick-start tips exclusively for you to show you how. You can access them at www.wealthcantwait.com /mastermind.

PART

**GENERATE THE MOMENTUM
THAT BUILDS WEALTH**

FIVE

CHAPTER 43

CREATE MOMENTUM THROUGH FLOW

People who succeed have momentum. The more they
succeed, the more they want to succeed, and the more
they find a way to succeed. Similarly, when someone is
failing, the tendency is to get on a downward spiral that
can become a self-fulfilling prophecy.
—Tony Robbins

Once you get a little wealth-building under your belt, you create
momentum and a state of flow. At the beginning of our wealth-building journey, it was all about hard work and generating as much value
for our company as we could. As our revenue increased, we began
to invest and build teams, and our worlds shifted from "I'll do it"
to "We'll do it." We became responsible for providing accountability,
creating a vision, and expanding our economic world to create new
opportunities for others.

The next step is to create the flow of wealth. Once you have moved
along the path of wealth building, then wealth becomes about flow.
The three most important types of flow are—

1. Deal flow
2. Talent flow
3. Life flow

Deal Flow

Once you build an area of expertise that generates revenue and asset appreciation, look for more deals and allow deals to flow through you. The more deals that flow through your pipeline, the more you see, the more you become aware of, the more you learn, and the better you become at using your gut and your brain to pick out the winners from the losers. It's a process of flow. Lots of deals flow by and you pick out the winners. It becomes natural and easy.

We use an opportunity matrix for evaluating deals. We look at the best-case scenario, the worst-case scenario, and the most-likely scenario. If the upside and most-likely scenarios are big enough, and we can live with downside should it happen, then the juice is worth the squeeze!

> " If the upside and most-likely scenarios are big enough, and we can live with downside should it happen, then the juice is worth the squeeze!"

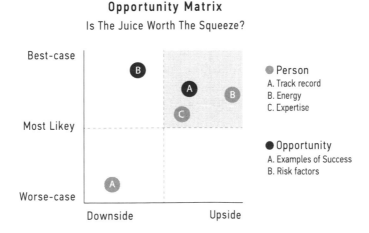

Figure 43.1

Talent Flow

Once you grasp the concept of people leverage and that no one succeeds alone, then you will begin to look for talent in all areas of your life. You'll constantly be on the lookout for great people who can take your business to higher levels of success or take on things in your personal life that will give you more time for your "one thing." This is called talent flow. People come and go in your life, and over time, you will add more and more talented people in key positions. Talented folks willing to buy into your vision of the future are key to taking your life to the next level. The talent could be doctors, lawyers, nannies, or employees. Or perhaps you want to attract talent to every area of your life.

> " Talented folks willing to buy into your vision of the future are key to taking your life to the next level."

If you have great talent, then it will also generate deal flow and talent flow for you. At that point, you truly are surfing a wave of abundance. You will still want to put your hand in the water to test the temperature, but now you're in a heightened state of abundance. You look at deal after deal and simply say "Yes" or "No," and your team handles the rest. This is a virtuous cycle of abundance.

Life Flow

Once you have the right deal-flow mechanisms around you and the right talent in place, then you can live anywhere in the world and keep in the flow. Simply tuning in, making a call, and then letting the great team you've hired take care of the rest of the details will suffice. At that point, you can choose to work 12-hour days or take 12 days off.

WEALTH ACCELERATOR

Building wealth is about creating sustainable deal flow, talent flow, and life flow.

CHAPTER 44

CREATE MOMENTUM THROUGH VIRTUOUS CYCLES

Success is like a snowball . . . It takes momentum to build,
and the more you roll in the right direction the bigger it gets.
—Steve Ferrante

The Five Strategies for Virtuous Cycles

Once you know that repeated behaviors are for the most part programs, you can begin to use that knowledge to reprogram yourself to wake up from destructive patterns and establish beneficial patterns that you repeat every day for a lifetime.

> " Once you know that repeated behaviors are for the most part programs, you can begin to use that knowledge to reprogram yourself to wake up from destructive patterns and establish beneficial patterns that you repeat every day for a lifetime."

If you had to take a guess of what David was up to on any given evening, you could assume he was partying. Why? Because it was a behavior that David carried forward from high school. Somehow he got into the mode of drinking a little too much and staying out a little too late and flirting a little too much. He then carried that pattern into his early career. It was a program.

When he thinks back on it, David's not sure he even enjoyed that lifestyle that much. It was just what he did. He remembers waking up with a hangover and putting himself in unsafe situations. It was a vicious cycle. If he hadn't stopped that cycle, it could have led to numerous problems and very poor health. One day he realized it just wasn't serving him anymore. He wanted more from life, and those late nights were not getting him there. So, he stopped. Today he is happy to be in bed by 10:00 p.m. He has a new pattern.

What patterns do you have? Are there any repeated actions you have that serve you? Are there any that don't?

Most of David's friends now love to exercise. No surprise they are all in very good shape. Two of David's colleagues are in their 50s and in great shape. He does a lot of business with both of these guys. It's common for them to interrupt business meetings to take a one-hour hike or to do pushups. They have a virtuous cycle embedded that keeps them moving their bodies, getting physical, exercising, and staying in shape. While this may be due to their programming, it's a great program that serves them well.

We all have virtuous and vicious cycles that we breathe life into. To succeed in life, we dump the vicious cycles and tune into the virtuous ones through these five strategies.

Strategy 1: Manage Your Relationships

Nothing affects our lives more than the people we hang out with. For example, if we hang out only with meat eaters, we won't likely be vegan. If our best friends drink every night, the odds are high that we will, too.

Maybe this seems harsh, but some of your friendships may be

holding you down instead of lifting you up. Think of it this way: One of the most important influences on children are their peers. If your kid is going down the wrong path as a teen, change schools. And if your life is not where you want it to be, change friendships.

David remembers when he was starting to achieve some success in business, one of his friends told him he was making him feel small because of his success. It hurt David to hear that. Pretty soon, though, he realized his friend did not want to stop playing video games or do more with his life. That wasn't enough for David, so he moved on.

Today, David chooses friends who either challenge him in business, health, or relationships, or are rocks of the earth—solid, dependable people who are taking care of their lives and making a difference each day. He also makes a point to surround himself with good peers who will help him be a better man, a better husband, and a better father.

Strategy 2: Create a Vision for Your Life

Use the online bonuses included in this book to help set a path you can commit to and set a course for your great future. It's not as daunting as you would think. Just make a plan and move toward it. Nothing is built without a set of plans. For example, no flights of any significance are made without a flight plan, and no great adventure is begun without a strategy. So, choose a path and review it regularly to make sure you are on track.

Strategy 3: Keep Learning

Never stop exposing yourself to new information, new ways of thinking, and new experiences. The minute you think you know it all, you begin to die. Children have incredible levels of curiosity. They never lose interest in new things, and this is why they learn so much. Their minds are like sponges, and their hearts are open and full of life. Don't let life beat that out of you. Most people love going to foreign countries. When we are walking down the boulevards of Paris, or the streets of Shanghai, our eyes are opened to new possibilities. We see the world in a new light, and that inspires our hearts and opens our minds. That state of mind is a creative and invigorating state. We should try to find that state daily.

Strategy 4: Hire a Coach

If you find that you cannot get in shape no matter how much you wish you could, hire a personal trainer. If you are not making the calls you need to make to build your business, hire an accountability coach. If you're still stuck on a relationship that doesn't work, hire a therapist. Lots of people have dedicated their lives to helping others. Hire those people. Let them use their passions and skills to help you put an end to any vicious cycles you have and add the power of virtuous momentum to your life.

Let us give you a real-world example. David has been intending to write the book you are now reading for more than five years. He was writing a lot but was also spinning his wheels (a vicious circle). He found that he kept forgetting what he'd written, or kept changing his mind about how he wanted the book to go. He even hired a ghostwriter at one point but didn't like the style of the book and felt it wasn't his own. So how did David break through?

First, he managed his relationships. When Paul mentioned he was intending to write a book on wealth, David decided to add Paul to create a virtuous relationship. Second, they began to meet to discuss where they were with the book, creating a feedback loop for the creative process. Third, after they had written quite a bit, they were still not where they wanted to be. So, they got together and tore the book apart, creating a vision for the book. Fourth, they constantly read new books and talked to authors to get ideas on how to do it right to create the best book possible. In other words, they kept on learning. Fifth, they hired a consultant to keep them moving in the right direction. And guess what? It worked. You are now reading a book that has been more than five years in the making!

Strategy 5: Do a Regular Life Audit

Just as we get physicals every year to check our cholesterol, our hearts, and our other bodily functions, we should also do a life audit to check the status of our relationships, the status of our families, and our life happiness index. It is hard to sleep our way through your life if we are always asking how it could get better. Ask yourself these questions and then live the answer. It is the question that has genius in it. If you have all the answers, how the heck are you going to remain curious and motivated to learn and experience more? The Life Audit practice is a crucial one that we'll guide you through in depth later in this book.

WEALTH ACCELERATOR

An old saying we love goes, "If you're digging in the wrong place, stop digging." In other words, if you see that you aren't where you want to be, not getting the results you want to have, and not moving in the direction you would like to move, then stop. Reevaluate your life and choose a new path—one that is empowering.

CHAPTER 45

CREATE MOMENTUM THROUGH SCALE

Growth is never by mere chance;
it is the result of forces working together.
—J. C. Penney

Wealth does not grow all at once. This is shortsighted and can lead to poor decisions. On the other hand, people quote the average annual increase in the stock market as if the average shareholder has one share of all the stocks in a particular index. Or they cite the average return on gold over ten years. Others think wealth is a long, continuous straight line into the future. But that isn't our experience.

Wealth grows in spurts and shrinks at times. Within every ten-year average, there are multiple (and possibly savings-busting) ups and downs. Some years your bounty will increase magnificently, and some will be flat or worse. Yet the ups and downs of the economy don't matter, if you follow the right strategy.

Plant Trees and Manage Orchards

" Wealth is built one good decision at a time."

Wealth is built one good decision at a time. Once you have erased your expensive consumer debt, learned to earn more, and have saved a bit, you can start planting money trees. A money tree is an asset that you purchase or invest in that pays you over time. A single-family rental property would be a good example of a money tree, as would recruiting a few people if you are at a profit-sharing company, investing in part of a multifamily property, or starting a small business. These are all examples of planting trees. Once you have a good number of money trees you manage your orchard.

David bought his first rental property in 1995. Today, he has nearly 100 single-family rentals and has invested in 2,000 apartment units. And Paul bought his first duplex in 1990 and now owns 700 rental units. It was a long process of building wealth. However, they added more wealth in the last three years than they did in the first ten years. It's a process of planting one tree at a time, and making good, solid decisions, one after another.

If it's a rental, make sure it works for cash flow. If you recruit, then don't stop: Keep adding people. If it's a multifamily investment and you are not the principal, then choose a principal with a great track record. Do your homework and learn enough about the model to understand the basics of the business. Don't base your investment decision solely on the information provided by the person wanting you to invest.

If you start a business, lead with revenue, not expenses, and learn how to be a great business owner and entrepreneur along the way. If you decide to invest in the stock market, then either study it or hire a great financial planner with a proven track record. And don't be afraid to ask tough questions.

Take the example of planting trees. What does the process look like? Most of the labor is up front: transporting the tree, digging the hole, planting the tree, and then refilling the hole. You give extra water, fertilizer, and lots of attention to a newly planted tree. After it takes root, then it's maintenance: You water the tree, pick the apples, and protect it from predators.

Making investments is the same: Do the work up front to be as certain as you can that you're making a good call. Study the fundamentals of the opportunity. Read up and then move to the next investment while looking back and learning from your previous experience: What did you do correctly and what would you change? Be a student. As you do that, reap the rewards, no matter how small. Then repeat the process.

> ❝ The extra time you spend upfront pays dividends in the end."

If you follow this strategy, nearly every subsequent decision that you make will be more solid than the previous decision. The extra time you spend upfront pays dividends in the end. These small investments may seem to go flat for a long time, but that won't matter because your investments won't require a boom to succeed. Designed for the long term, they'll be able to sustain a declining market. And then when a boom comes, you will reap the benefits of your good investment decisions.

For instance, when the real estate bust hit in 2008, a lot of people lost fortunes in real estate, but our portfolios were unscathed. Because our properties were not overleveraged, they produced enough cash flow to continue to pay all the bills and then some. Our tenants didn't read the dismal economic news and say, "I'm not paying my rent." Instead, they paid their rent no matter what. And in spite of, or even because of, the economy, the demand for basic, safe, clean, and inexpensive rentals in good areas went up. In fact, because we had been conservative during the early 2000s when the market was booming, we had extra capital saved up, which we deployed in 2010–2012.

We recommend making one good decision after another. At some point, as you keep planting, you will gather enough momentum to make a substantial financial difference for yourself and your family. The assets you have invested in will bloom, and then they will boom. And your wealth will get an enormous boost because of all the work you have done in the years before. When this happens, people around you who didn't do the work will say, "Wow, he's a lucky guy!" And you know what? It will be true!

Manage Orchards

As we invest in more and more assets, we will begin to have an orchard, meaning that we'll have more and more assets that bear fruit. Once we reach this stage, we have to learn how to manage orchards. At some point, our world gets too big for us to handle it all. At that point, management skills kick in. Management skills mean that we learn to leverage through people talent and systems talent. It's easier in many ways to manage a collection of assets than to play just one. Most of the management can be outsourced.

Keep this in mind: The effort it takes to plant one tree when analyzed against the small return you'll get from it in the few years to come is discouraging. It's why most people look at folks who own and manage orchards and fail to be inspired. They look across the street and see a massive orchard as they toil to plant a single tree and wonder: Do they continue or just forget it? Paul didn't imagine he would own 700 apartment units when he went through all the trouble and risk of buying his first duplex, but he kept growing his orchard, one tree at a time. And you can, too.

WEALTH ACCELERATOR

You plant trees one at a time, but you manage orchards to build great wealth. Start planting now!

CHAPTER 46

CREATE MOMENTUM THROUGH HEALTH

When asked how to increase productivity, Sir Richard Branson replied with two words: "Work out." Timothy Ferriss goes on to summarize Branson's rationale by stating: "Working out gave him at least four additional hours of productive time every day."

How is health related to wealth? It's simple. Wealth is as much a function of health as anything. If you look at the *Forbes* list of wealthiest people, you will notice one thing: There are a lot of senior citizens on the list. Living a long time facilitates the power of compounding. In addition to the power of compounding, wealth can also be a reflection of vitality. It makes sense that increased energy combined with advancing skillsets magnify your outcome and amplify your income! There is no better way to increase your energy and productivity than taking great care of your health.

Magnify your outcome and amplify your income! There is no better way to increase your energy and productivity than taking great care of your health.

> " In addition to the power of compounding, wealth can also be a reflection of vitality."

In fact, the original meaning of the word wealth comes from Middle English "wele" or well-being. Wealth is an analogy of health. We are literally our own temple. We have one body. It will serve us for our lifetime no matter how we treat it. So how about treating it as if it were the only one we're going to have?

It takes awareness to stay healthy in today's world. The Western diet is deficient. Use your awareness before you eat. As often as possible, choose foods that support your body. An empowered physical state will serve to enhance your mental and material states. When in doubt, go closer to nature and eat fresher, more-authentic natural foods.

Your Environment Must Support Your Health Goals

People say, "You are what you eat." The reality is, you are what you buy at the grocery store. If it is in your house, the odds are you will eat it at some point. So, develop an environment that supports your goals. In our houses, we keep a lot of fresh vegetables, fresh fruit, raw nuts, and some dried fruits. Our snacks most often come from these sources. We aren't trying to be perfect. We keep some unhealthy snacks around, like a small container of ice cream or sorbet, a dark chocolate bar, and some ginger snaps. We are not totalitarians when it comes to our food. We just have an 80/20 ratio of healthy foods to those that are questionable. This means that we tend to snack on the healthier side of the equation.

Interestingly enough, David has permanently lost a dozen pounds since he shifted to this outlook. The other ironic thing is that the healthier your diet, the more you start to crave healthier foods. David added a rule to eat a salad at the beginning of most meals even when he didn't want one. Now if he goes a couple of days without a salad, he starts craving fresh greens—something he never did as a child.

Of course, part of your environment is where you live. David was going to move to Los Angeles in 2001 for a business venture. But when he got there, he would look out the window of his hotel every morning and see a yellow haze of smog and pollution over the valley. It was clear to him that he could never live in Los Angeles. So, he decided to commute instead and still does today.

In 2004, he bought a place in Colorado where he could ski and bike. Now he skis 20–30 times a year. Every time he gets back to Texas, his legs are stronger, his heart is healthier, and his attitude and mind are more robust. Why? Because he lives in an environment that supports his goal of increased health.

Your Tribe Must Support Your Health Goals

Staying in incredible shape does not come naturally to David. He didn't start off as an athlete of any significance. He was not raised in a nutritionally conscious family. Kraft macaroni and cheese and spaghetti were favorite meals at home. His parents were practical people who grew up during World War II with an industrial-age mindset. David had no predisposition or family training in the area of health.

His dad was pretty decent at working out. Though he was fit and a retired Green Beret, he never insisted that David work out, so David never really developed that habit until later. But as he grew older, he added a precious dimension to his health—a tribe of great friends and peers to whom being in shape was incredibly important.

Some of the guys he hangs out with are very committed to going the extra mile when it comes to health. They are skiers, mountain bikers, and trail runners. When they get together, there is a lot of working out that goes along with the companionship. They go on annual adventure trips. So far, they have climbed Mount Kilimanjaro and Mount Whitney and hiked part of the Appalachian Trail. Each year they get together to do something physical.

So, guess what happens a couple of months before the trip? David's workouts kick up to a whole new level, because when he gets together with them, he doesn't want to be the guy who can't keep up. His tribe motivates him to stay in shape. If your tribe is in the beer-swilling, cheesecake-munching, movie-watching, sedentary-living clan, we suggest you seek out a new tribe.

A Big Why

Health is important to us. Do you have a big why for committing to age-defying health? If you are not one of those few who naturally craves fitness, use your big why to make a choice toward health. For us it's simple: We have chosen to have children at a later stage in life. Paul has a daughter who will graduate high school when he is 56, and David has a son who will graduate high school when he is 67. When their children graduate, they would still like to be able to participate in their lives. So, they work out as much for their relationship with their kids as they do for themselves.

That's a pretty big why. What's yours?

WEALTH ACCELERATOR

Wealth is synonymous with health. Work out to increase your energy and your earnings.

CHAPTER 47

CREATE MOMENTUM THROUGH ENVIRONMENT

You are a product of your environment. So, choose the
environment that will best develop you toward your
objective. Analyze your life in terms of its environment.
Are the things around you helping you toward success—
or are they holding you back?
—W. Clement Stone

The environment we live in will either support our health or destroy
it. The environment we work in can stimulate growth or stunt it.
The environment we come home to can enhance our life or squelch
it. That's why it is so important to protect and nourish our personal
environment.

A business environment that supports our goals is an environment
filled with positive, make-it-happen people, a talented and supportive
administrative staff, an office designed just the way we like it, the right
people working with us, and a great industry that we love. A great
business environment has plenty of lead generation, plenty of cash
flow, excellent financial reporting, and high accountability.

What does a home environment that supports our goals look like?
For David, it's a house full of healthy food. It seems like every day

around 4:00 p.m. he wants to snack on something unhealthy. Guess what? He only has healthy food available his house. So, where he used to go and eat chips, now he eats an apple. What was once Snickers is now dark chocolate. The difference in how he feels after eating these foods is enormous.

Your sleeping space should be calm, free from electronics, dark, and cool, promoting rest and sound sleep. David's bedroom is dark, quiet, and free of distractions. It is designed for rest and recovery. David chose to live in a clean city where outdoor activities are easy to do, where hiking, biking, and healthy living are not a battle against traffic, smog, and heat.

It's also very important is to avoid working for a company that squelches innovation and personal growth. Don't work for an organization that sabotages your desire for a greater future. Instead, work somewhere that celebrates expansion, embraces balance, and encourages living large. You spend a large portion of your life at work, so choose that environment wisely.

> " Don't work for an organization that sabotages your desire for a greater future. Instead, work somewhere that celebrates expansion, embraces balance, and encourages living large."

And lastly, if you don't love your car, get one that you do love. If you don't love your home, move somewhere else. If you don't love your lifestyle, change it. Wear the clothes that feel right to you. Sleep in a bed that comforts and supports you. Everything is energy. Create the environment that brings you the most energy possible. You don't have tons of money. You can create an amazing environment on a tight budget. The money you spend will be well worth it.

WEALTH ACCELERATOR

Create an environment that supports your goals and growth. And be disciplined about maintaining that environment every day and everywhere you go.

TAKE ACTION AND BEGIN YOUR LIFE AUDIT

Your purpose in life is to find your purpose
and give your whole heart and soul to it.
—Gautama Buddha

Are Your Actions Getting You Where and What You Want?

This is the critical question that is so easily overlooked. However, once you start asking and answering this question, you begin taking the actions that will change and improve your life. That's where the Life Audit comes in. It's your tuning fork to home in on what is happening right now. A Life Audit will help you discover—

- Where you are
- If you are where you planned to be
- Where you want to be

Think of the Life Audit as a balance sheet of your life, a snapshot of right now. This is vital because for you to choose where you want your future to go, you have to know where you are today. What's the first question you would ask someone who asked for directions to your house? Likely it would be, "Where are you now?" That way you would have perspective on which way they would need to go to get to your house.

David has had a high-level accountability group for nearly 20 years. When they started, they never called their process a Life Audit. They simply started building the outcomes they wanted and held each other accountable for fulfilling them. As time went on, when they got back together or talked on the phone, their accountability partner would want to know where they were at that moment. In other words, they wanted to know how their plans were manifesting. Eventually, they created a system where they discussed—

- Their past goals
- The outcomes of their goals
- The effect these outcomes had on their lives
- Their present condition (the Life Audit)
- Their plan to keep moving forward in their chosen direction

As this format evolved, they chose tools from various sources that fixed these techniques into their behavior, which they now use every time they have their face-to-face masterminds, which are usually twice a year.

Performing a Life Audit through the process we describe here is essentially taking stock of your life by breaking it down into the categories that are important to you and then assessing where you are relative to where you would like to be.

For example, you might be in great shape but be unhappy in your career. Or like Paul, you might wish you had a more developed spiritual life. The Life Audit is a great starting point. We love this exercise, because it offers a guarantee of the best return on your investment.

Life Audit Tool 1: The Life Happiness Index

The Life Happiness Index allows you to break your life into important sectors and raises your awareness of each of the sectors. We suggest focusing on the following areas:

1. Personal
2. Family
3. Health/Physical
4. Health/Mental
5. Spiritual
6. Social
7. Career
8. Charity
9. Community service
10. Marriage/Relationship
11. Education/Continuing education
12. Recreation
13. Vacation
14. Other personal development

You can also add "roles" that are specific to your world like dad/mom, husband/wife, employer/employee, and so forth. By breaking your life into sectors, you can add energy where you want to improve your life. That's why we consider the Life Happiness Index a tool to get a higher return on investment. We can implement systems and education around the areas in our lives that need the most attention.

Here's what the Life Happiness Index looks like.

Life Happiness Index
Where Am I Now?

Don't sleepwalk through your life. Be aware of where you are on or off track.
On a 1-10 scale, rate yourself on how well you are fulfilling each category.

	1ST QUARTER	2ND QUARTER	3RD QUARTER	4TH QUARTER
Diet, Water				
Exercise				
DPA (Dollar Production Activities				
Love for Work				
Romance				
Children				
Parents, Siblings, etc.				
Friends				
Horizontal Income				
Music & Dance				
Hobbies				
Adventure, Travel				
Risk & Excitement				
Chill Time				
Giving Back				
Future Planning				
Gratitude Thermometer				
LHI AVERAGE				
Weight				
Body Fat%				
Blood Pressure				
Life Expectancy				
Biological Age				

Figure 48.1

" The Life Happiness Index is a way to integrate all the tools that follow into one master dashboard that tracks your health and happiness."

The Life Happiness Index is a way to integrate all the tools that follow into one master dashboard that tracks your health and happiness. "Biological Age," referred to in the Life Happiness Index form, is sponsored by the Harpo Network, the Discovery Channel, and Sony, and features Dr. Oz and a battery of health experts. You'll need to go to your physician beforehand, because the assessment asks for test results in addition to all of the lifestyle questions that you might expect.

Life Audit Tool 2: The Financial Statement

Every time you apply for a loan or credit, you usually have to fill one of these out. If you play the Cash Flow Quadrant Classic Game, they use a financial statement. They don't teach this financial statement in high school. Even if you learn it in college, you rarely use it except when you are getting credit.

But if you choose to approach and build wealth with purpose, then your financial statement is a scoreboard of your financial life. If you truly want to build wealth, then it's important for you to have a working familiarity with your balance sheet, your wins and losses. You don't have to have a master's in accounting or pass a CPA exam. But you do have to know how to work your balance sheet.

Life Audit Tool 3: Horizontal Income Statement

This is the centerpiece of our strategy. We use horizontal income to forecast the income of any assets we purchase. Ultimately, we all end up living off some form of horizontal income—social security, 401(k) s, savings, investments, retirement plans, or dividend income. Ideally, multiple streams of income from multiple sources.

How much vertical income you make annually—whether $20,000 a year or $1 million a year—is irrelevant as it pertains to your future. If you make $1 million a year for five years but don't create horizontal income, all you can say is that you had five great years and a great lifestyle at that time.

But we who are committed to horizontal income think about finances this way:

Gross Income - Taxes - All Essential Expenses - Fun Living Expenses = Discretionary Income, which is money left to invest.

The fundamental steps to consider when creating horizontal income sources are—

1. Gain awareness: Most people are unaware of the need for a horizontal income plan.
2. Create a plan.
3. Be accountable to the plan.
4. Repeat the steps.

One of the easiest ways to accomplish multiple streams of income, paid monthly, is through real estate. For example—

- Buy a house that has cash flow potential with 20-30% down.
- Monthly rent pays the mortgage. (Consider 15-year mortgages for faster pay down.)
- Income over and above the mortgage and other associated expenses becomes your first few hundred horizontal income bucks.
- Save the profits.
- Repeat the process.
- To determine real estate investment cash flow—

- Take the gross rent and deduct 40% for vacancy, management fees, taxes, insurance, and repairs.
- With 60% left over, deduct principle and interest.
- The amount remaining is your free cash flow.
- Target properties in the middle to lower economic zones for cash flow. Targeting high-end properties is riskier and is more of an appreciation play.

You can track your real estate investment cash flow with the following chart.

Horizontal Income

	1ST QUARTER	2ND QUARTER	3RD QUARTER	4TH QUARTER	TOTAL
Earned Income					
RENTALS					
Various Rental Expenses					
Total Rentals					
NOTES					
Total Notes					
FLIPPERS					
Net Flipper Income					
MISC.					
Total Misc. Income					
TOTAL INCOME					
Personal Expenses					
Income Left to Invest					
OTHER INCOME					
Pension					
Social Security					
Dividends					
Stocks					
Total Other Income					
Total Income					

Figure 48.3

Life Audit Tool 4: Budget and Income

Dave Ramsey teaches that we should give each dollar a mission. He's right. You have to get a handle on where you're spending your dollars. You should think of each dollar as a potential income generator. If you invest your dollars wisely in horizontal-income opportunities, then over your lifetime, if you're wise, those dollars could multiply many times over. So, your budget (which doesn't have to be perfect) is your management strategy for your future income generators. You will see one difference in our budget over the standard budget forms out there. We don't have a net column or a savings column. Instead, we have a line item that says "left over to invest." We use this language to put into perspective how we see leftover cash and to help you develop the mindset of the financially free.

Life Audit Tool 5: More of/Less of

66 As you build wealth and success, you will learn that you make the most money and have the most success when you do more of what you're good at and love to do and less of what you're not good at and don't love to do."

As you build wealth and success, you will learn that you make the most money and have the most success when you do more of what you're good at and love to do and less of what you're not good at and don't love to do. It's a simple and empowering idea. The more of/less of graph looks like this:

GOOD AT AND LOVE	GOOD AT AND HATE
BAD AT AND LOVE	BAD AT AND HATE

The happiest and therefore most successful people put themselves in the good-at-and-love quadrant as much as possible. That's why you hear successful people saying things like, "I don't see it as work. It's more like play to me." These are people who say they'll never retire. People that leave a mark in life, who love getting up on Monday and going to work. Expressions like "I hate Mondays" and "Thank God it's Friday" don't hold sway over them. In fact, those expressions mean nothing to these people.

People who put themselves in the good-at-and-love quadrant end up having a calling, not a job. They end up living in a world they love. This is true not just for work but in all areas of their lives.

You can successfully bring the practice of "more of/less of" into every area of your life, too. For example, ask yourself—

- What would you like more of and less of at home?
- What would you like more of and less of in the area of physical health?
- What would you like more of and less of in your spiritual life?
- What would you like more of and less of in your personal life?

Just asking these questions brings awareness, and with it more choice.

❝ Moving toward things you want and away from things you don't is an empowering, fulfilling process.❞

Moving toward things you want and away from things you don't is an empowering, fulfilling process. It's fun and creates a higher standard of living for you and those around you. It leads to better health, wealth, and relationships if you let it.

Here is an exercise for you. Take a blank piece of paper and write the subject at the top. For example, consider health:

Health

MORE OF	LESS OF
Sleep	Sugar
Yoga	Alcohol

WEALTH ACCELERATOR

Create a more of/less of chart for every life area. It's a brief but powerful exercise. If you do this purposefully once a month, it will change everything for the better.

Life Audit Tool 6: The Five-Year Vision

If you start with the end in mind, then it is important for you to have a vision for your life. We use several tools to do this. One of our favorites is the five-year vision, which is simply a written summary of the next five years as if they had already occurred. We've included a sample five-year vision in the online bonus for this appendix.

Life Audit Tool 7: Someday Goals

Sticking with the theme of starting with the end in mind, we keep open-ended someday goals. For instance, a sample someday goal for the family could be—

A large, loving, well-adjusted family of healthy individuals who pursue their own goals, live their lives on purpose, and support and love one another on the journey.

See the someday goal as a mission statement or vision statement for each quadrant of your life, including health, wealth, and contribution.

Life Audit Tool 8: One-Year Goals

For us, this is where the rubber hits the road. Think of these areas as gardens. And just like a real garden, they need tending. Each year David sets one-year goals in the following areas:

- Relationship/Family
- Spiritual/Contribution
- Physical/Nutrition
- Intellectual/Education
- Lifestyle/Adventure
- Environment/Tribe
- Business financial goals

Then he develops his one-year goals for each of his business ventures in coordination with the guys that run them for him. Because he is so committed to hitting his goals, his life manifests abundantly in the areas he chooses. This simple activity has become an empowering habit in David's life. As he's developed the ability to set and accomplish his goals, his life has improved exponentially in many areas. And yours can, too!

Life Audit Tool 9: Power Questions

When we go on our adventure masterminds, among the things we bring with us are what we call Power Questions. We come up with questions that stimulate both the mind and the spirit. Questions that help each person think of new possibilities for their lives. Think of it as a first creation (in the mind) and a second creation (in the world around us).

We have more than 100 Power Questions that we're going to make available as an online bonus for you, but to whet your appetite, here are four Power Question sets that can put you on track to a strong, purposeful future.

1. In your limitless future, what is the ideal way you would contribute to the world with your time?

2. In that someday future, how do you see your daily life flowing?

3. In that same limitless future (say, 10 or even 20 years in the future), is your world financed? What does your horizontal (passive) income look like? How many sources of horizontal income do you have?

4. What are your key intention statements for the following areas of your life: health, family, business/income, contribution/making a difference, and personal development?

Life Audit Tool 10: Dream Boards

Not only is it fun to make a dream board with your loved one or family members, it can also be a strong visual reminder of the future you are crafting for yourself. Here is one that David's wife, Traci, created for him in 2006. It has given him and his subconscious a visual reminder of where he is sending the clay of his life.

How Often Should You Do a Life Audit?

You don't have to obsess over your future. It is certainly going to come, whatever you do. We recommend doing your Life Audits at least once per year. David has gotten into the habit of doing his twice a year at his face-to-face masterminds. Find a timeframe that works for you and stick to it. The important thing is that you conduct one and revisit it. The purpose of this is twofold: One, it helps you stay focused on your goals. And two, it can also be inspiring to see how many you have already accomplished, which can lead to the creation of newer, bigger goals.

Who Are the Wealthiest among Us, and Do They Use Life Audits?

Who has the greatest wealth? Hedge fund managers, Warren Buffett, real estate tycoons? Do you think any of these types of people operate without an awareness of—

- Where their money is going? (A budget)
- How much income they have and from what sources? (A horizontal income statement)
- How much they have in cash and assets and how much they owe? (A balance sheet)
- A plan for the investments they make (Goal: 15-Year Vision)

Of course not. They are on top of all of these things at all times. They also have a plan for their cash. Learn from them and create healthy financial habits that will benefit you for years to come.

Some people make huge amounts of money with limited financial skills, but this is rare. If you watch the biographies of rock stars and athletes who fit this profile, it is amazing how many of them lose all their money at least once. Often their financial managers steal all their money. If you are a regular person, the odds of building wealth without a plan go down massively.

WEALTH ACCELERATOR

Having a plan for your financial future dramatically increases the likelihood of your financial success. You cannot set a course for a future destination without knowing where you are today. A Life Audit defines your destination so you can plot your course to a financially free future.

BONUS CONTENT: TOMORROW STARTS TODAY

To help inspire you further as you plan for the life of your dreams, we're sharing some bonus content with you. By visiting wealthcantwait.com/tomorrowstartstoday, you will be able to access Paul's Dream Budgets, A Sample Five-Year Vision, and our Complete List of 100 Power Questions. What are you waiting for? Start planning your tomorrow today!

ABOUT THE AUTHORS

DAVID OSBORN was raised in Europe, educated in Great Britain, and completed his studies in 1990 at the University of Texas at Austin majoring in Economics. David's real estate career took off shortly after he opened his first Keller Williams brokerage in the mid-1990s. He is presently the principal owner in the 20th largest real estate company in the US with 2,100+ agents responsible for more than 19,000 transaction sides and $4.5 billion in sales in 2015. He is an operating principal and or/investor in five Keller Williams Regions and nine Market Centers.

In addition to owning regions and brokerages, David is the principal of a private equity group that has bought and sold approximately 1,000 homes. He owns more than 1,500 apartment units, office, retail, and industrial buildings. His group has bought and sold tens of millions in notes and distressed assets, improved the quality of the assets, sold them for profit, or retained them for cash flow. He is a primary investor or operator of more than 35 profitable real estate–related businesses and currently does, or has done, business in more than 40 states and Canada.

Firmly rooted to the principle of knowledge-sharing and giving back, David is a member of the Keller Williams Master Faculty and regularly teaches as a keynote speaker. He is a founder and operating partner of GoBundance, an accountability-based group of hard-charging, generous entrepreneurs living exceptional lives. Further, David sits on the board of the One Life Fully Lived non-profit, is a member of YPO/WPO Austin, and TIGER 21, and contributes to various causes—from fighting cancer to building clean-water wells through Charity Water. David is the proud father of two beloved daughters and one amazing son and is married to the wonderful and talented Traci Osborn.

PAUL MORRIS is a prolific and award-winning entrepreneur, trainer, author, and business consultant. As an active investor, he has grown his real estate portfolio to more than 700 rental units and 150,000 square feet of commercial retail space. In ten years, he transformed his California-based real estate brokerage business into the second largest Keller Williams franchise, with ten offices employing 2,200 agents. *Real Trends* ranked his group the thirty-sixth largest real estate brokerage in the United States, having closed $3.6 billion in real estate sales in 2012. Before working full-time in real estate, Paul had a successful legal career, highlighted by his work as an associate at Proskauer Rose, a New York–based international firm, and as Senior Counsel for the US Department of Justice. Paul graduated *magna cum laude* in economics from the University of Pittsburgh, has a master's degree in Management from Oxford University, and a JD from Cornell Law School.

AUTHOR Q&A

Is there an end goal to building wealth, or should an individual always build wealth no matter how much they already have?

Paul Morris: There is this underlying presumption that building wealth is somehow in some way a sacrifice. That's what stops people from building wealth to begin with. If building wealth were inside a labor of love, would you stop when you hit a certain number? I am not naïve: Building wealth is a discipline that requires effort and awareness. It is not always easy. But as I create more wealth, I adjust: I outsource more of what I don't love to do (which in turn increases my productivity, passion, and love for my work). Over time, as I get better at the things I focus on, my specific advantage grows: I can do more in less time with less effort. The power required to launch, if it's a big enough life, can be enormous. But once you have momentum and lift, flight itself requires far less energy and can take you where you want to go.

David Osborn: A: Our definition of wealth, the original meaning, means health, wealth, and prosperity. You can never have too much health and prosperity, so my answer is no. Personal development never stops.

What is the ideal time/age to start building wealth?

Morris: The best time to start is sometime in the distant past. Since we cannot change the past, however, our real choices are to start building wealth right now or sometime in the future. Choose now! It does not matter how old or how young you are—there is always possibility and right now is *the* best time to start.

Osborn: There is no better time than now, the earlier you start the easier it is . . . but it's never too late.

Did you have a wealth vision when you started out? What did it look like?

Morris: The wealth we have now is a product of our wealth vision, whether we think we have one or not. By consciously considering that vision—writing it out, editing it, reflecting on it, working toward it—we can exert greater control over it. It's important to stop and ask yourself: "What do I think my future will be like?" And, powerfully, "What would my future look like if I had 100% control over it?"

Before I was purposeful about building wealth, I would have answered, "I have no 'wealth vision.'" Being purposeful increases the degree of control we have over our future. So, in the beginning I had two visions: what I would love my future to be (I have far exceeded that "wish"), and what I actually thought it would be. At a time when I had no purposeful vision, I used the things I didn't like—a job I hated, a time-clock I had to punch, places I "had" to go but didn't want to go—and thought, it would be amazing if I had enough wealth that I didn't *have* to do what I didn't *want* to do.

The more that I thought about it, the more I began to realize that wealth equaled freedom, among other things. And, I began to build toward a life that had more freedom. In the beginning, though, I thought I had no wealth vision. Now I realize it's better to create that vision in a purposeful way. After I had already built wealth and spent time thinking about it (more of a middle ground), I took all of my expenses and thought "what would it be like to live this really nice life and have enough passive income to cover it?" That was well after I had begun to build wealth but also the beginning of really using vision to build wealth.

Osborn: My original vision was to own ten rentals fully paid for, purchase one every year, and put them on 15-year leases. I was 30 when I put that down on paper. At 55 I would have had ten fully paid-for rentals and I estimated $100K per year after expenses.

You each built your wealth in a very successful real estate company. Do you feel real estate is an ideal industry in which to build wealth? What are some other successful wealth-building industries?

Morris: People generally get "paid" for having a specific advantage. That means knowing the market better than average. If you know a particular industry better than the market knows it, it will be a fertile place to build wealth. You gain a specific advantage by building expertise. Building expertise can be incredibly difficult and painful or absolute joy or somewhere in between. Do what you truly love and you will build expertise with ease. That said, I do believe that real estate is a particularly easy-to-learn market that we can all win in over time with discipline and energy devoted to the right places. I can say that with certainty, irrespective of market cycles, where I cannot say that for any other industry.

Osborn: There have been more millionaires created through real estate than any other industry in the history of the world. As the old saying goes: "Don't wait to buy real estate, buy real estate and wait." However owning and operating businesses, if mastered, can be not only profitable but highly educational. There are many ways to succeed in life; the key is to pick an industry and get into mastery.

What made you choose to write about building wealth as an overall concept rather than discuss your journeys and successes in real estate specifically?

Morris: The lessons that helped me succeed in real estate are, for the most part, life lessons. My journey is more about learning how to succeed—changing my mindset and opening my perspective—than it is about learning the specifics of the real estate industry. In fact, I find the specifics of "making it in real estate" to be a bit of a bore and a footnote to the amazing, magnificent journey that becoming a great adult/dad/partner/businessperson has been and continues to be.

Osborn: The principles of wealth building work anywhere. I have built more wealth through operating businesses than through ownership of real estate.

Both of you travel and conduct business internationally. Is there a difference in the ideas or abilities of building wealth in other countries?

Morris: I have not built wealth internationally. I know that succeeding at a high level requires understanding a culture deeply and creating advantage inside of that particular system. The same is true nationally: Different sensibilities reign in different parts of our own country. For example, a style of negotiation, project management, or project completion that works on the east coast might not do as well on the west coast or in the southern US.

Osborn: America is one of, if not the best place to build wealth. However, almost every concept in this book will allow you to build wealth anywhere.

What would you say is the most important message or concept in this book?

Morris: Anyone can do it; not everyone will. If you want to change your external circumstances, you must first change your internal mindset. Here's a metaphor that I use and believe in: The overweight man finally becomes thin not after years of diet and exercise—those will fail when he reverts back to his real self—but immediately after he decides to *be* thin. Once that decision to be thin is made with 100% certainty, the person is already thin: It just takes a little while to manifest. A diet that is not from the inside out will be fleeting—if it works in the first place—because the body will revert to its true form, and that is the form that is created and maintained from within. So, the most important part of the book—and I never knew it or would have agreed until later in life—is the beginning of the book and that is the mindset of wealth.

Osborn: Wealth building is accomplished by personal development. As you grow, your wealth will grow.

What is the most practical way to earn the capital to start building wealth?

Morris: There are three ways that I know of, and I have used them all. The first is to earn a bit more than you spend. In the beginning this is the hardest and least effective in the short term. However, it is also the most certain—so use it! The second is to use other people's capital. You have to earn their trust and have a unique skill set. Very early in my career, I partnered with a real estate agent and my best friend to find an opportunity to invest in multifamily real estate that had higher yields than other very safe investments. We took this to friends and family who did not have the access and the knowledge that we had and we used our time and effort as our contribution. And, the third is to use a combination of skill and effort to earn equity at something you are very good at. I have done this successfully and unsuccessfully throughout my career. I did this as a COO of a failed Internet start-up—I used the salary to pay my bills and took a shot at a big upside (which never happened) if the company took off. I did this as a lawyer—I charged half my hourly rate to help fledgling companies form and get funded and then took two to three times my hourly rate in stock in their companies. And I also did this in the brokerage firms that I own—at first being the "working" partner earning equity and salary as compensation, and eventually doing the same for talented folks on my team who get paid and bonused in equity.

Osborn: Being the best at something you love is the best way to earn capital. However, you can do deals with other people's capital . . . and that requires excellence in stewardship and results, and not a great deal of capital.

When discussing thinking easy vs. thinking hard, you mentioned how you felt finishing this book was hard. What was the most difficult aspect of writing this book, and how did you overcome it?

Morris: Everyone is different, so everyone enjoys and is naturally talented in certain areas and naturally challenged in others. My greatest gift/obstacle is impatience. My lack of attention span leads me to leave projects—especially long ones that require a lot of sitting still—"mostly done." I am so impatient I find it terribly difficult to read books. So, taking the time to sit still long enough to think, write, edit, rethink, etc., was difficult. I loved the idea of writing the book and even loved the process, but I also would grow tired of it and wanted to move on before it was good enough to have the great value it could have for our potential readers. I had to see the greater good and dig deep to complete the process.

Osborn: Writing it the first time wasn't hard. It was editing it the tenth to fifteenth times time that I found hard. I overcame it by building a great team, having accountability with my coauthor, and envisioning the final outcome to stay motivated.

What is the number-one mistake people make on their wealth-building journey?

Morris: The number-one mistake that most people make is being too afraid to begin, or too afraid of making a mistake. In reality, they should fear doing nothing a lot more. The tricky part is evaluating where you are and who you are before you figure that out. If you have thought about it but never done anything about it, then *doing* is the biggest thing—just do it. If you have already started and failed many times, then starting is not your issue—what is most important to this person is different. Most often, though, the mistake is not starting. The second-largest mistake is not sticking with what will eventually work—giving up too soon. As real estate experts, David and I know we cannot predict the very top or very bottom of a market. I invest less aggressively and more carefully when the market is "near" the top and invest more aggressively when the market is "near" the bottom. Here is the problem when you are actually doing it: The mindset of investment runs in the opposite direction. When the market is near the top, all headlines read of amazing moneymaking stories. It's easier to jump in. When the market is near the bottom, the headlines read as if global economic crisis—the likes of which we have never seen—is right around the corner. It is tough to have the skin to buy when the papers say it's so bad out there.

Osborn: The biggest mistake is not starting it soon enough. Waiting too long, and finding to many reasons not to take action.

What has been the most rewarding aspect of writing this book?

Morris: Despite all that I have said above, I don't sit still that well. Writing it has given me a chance to give form to the many, many ideas swirling in my head. It has been a discipline I would not have otherwise done. We've produced something we are both very happy and proud of. The book will be a contribution to those around us who can learn from the many fits and starts that we have had. Hopefully it will make their journeys easier or even possible where they otherwise would not be. I want to give one person the courage to start who otherwise would not have started and inspire them to make it big—very big, maybe bigger than David and I make it in our journeys. That would be super cool.

Osborn: It's rewarding to think that my great-grandkids could pick up this book and learn something that might make their lives a little more fulfilling.

Are either of you considering any new wealth-building business ventures for the future?

Morris: I am staying the course a while until I take real estate to the next level. There is so much in this industry that I have created a great launching pad for but have not yet realized. That will be my focus for the next bit of my professional career. And, all the while, I'll be creating and living in a space that is more and more fun for me, and allows me to do more of what I love and what I am passionate about, while outsourcing the rest. Wow, that sounds fun, energizing, and profitable. Let the next chapter begin!

Osborn: I recently started a private equity fund. And I am very excited about building it.